Tertullian

Against Praxeas

Tertullian

Against Praxeas

Tertullian
Against Praxeas

Published by
Lighthouse Christian Publishing
SAN 257-4330
5531 Dufferin Drive
Savage, Minnesota, 55378
United States of America

www.lighthousechristianpublishing.com

Tertullian

Introductory Note.

The Second Class of Tertullian's works, according to the logical method I have endeavored to carry out, is that which includes his treatises against the heresies of his times. In these, the genius of our author is brilliantly illustrated, while, in melancholy fact, he is demonstrating the folly of his own final lapse and the wickedness of that schism and heresy into which he fell away from Truth. Were it not that history abounds in like examples of the frailty of the human intellect and of the insufficiency of "man that walketh to direct his steps," we should be forced to a theory of mental decay to account for inconsistencies so gross and for delusions so besotted. "Genius to madness is *indeed* allied," and who knows but something like that imbecility which closed the career of Swift may have been the fate of this splendid wit and versatile man of parts? Charity, admiration and love force this inquiry upon my own mind continually, as I explore his fascinating pages. And the order in which the student will find them in this series, will lead, I think, to similar reflections on the part of many readers. We observe a natural bent and turn of mind, even in his Catholic writings, which indicate his perils. These are more and more apparent in his recent works, as his enthusiasm heats itself into a frenzy which at last becomes a rage. He breaks down by degrees, as in orthodoxy so also in force and in character. It is almost like the collapse of Solomon or of Bacon. And though our own times have produced no example of stars of equal magnitude, to become falling-stars, we have seen illustrations the most humiliating, of those calm words of Bishop Kaye: "Human nature often presents the curious phenomenon of a union of the most opposite qualities in the same mind; of vigor, acuteness and discrimination on some subjects, with imbecility, dullness and bigotry on others." Milton, himself another example of his own threnode, breaks forth in this splendid utterance of lyrical confession:

> "God of our fathers what is man?
> Nor do I name of men the common rout,
> That, wandering loose about,
> Grow up and perish as the summer fly,
> Heads without name, no more remembered,
> But such as thou hast solemnly elected,
> With gifts and graces eminently adorned,
> To some great work, thy glory
> And people's safety, *which in part they effect*."

And here, I must venture a remark on the ambiguity of the expressions concerning our author's Montanism. In the treatise against Marcion, written late in his career, Tertullian identifies himself with the Church and strenuously defends its faith and its apostolic order. In only rare instances does his weakness for the "new prophecy" crop out, and then, it is only as one identifies himself with a school within the church. Precisely so Fenelon maintained his milder Montanism, without a thought of deserting the Latin Church. Afterwards Fenelon drew back, but at last poor Tertullian fell away. So with the Jansenists. They credited the *miracles* and the *convulsions* (or ecstasies) of their school, and condemned those who rejected them, as Tertullian condemns the *Psychics*. The great expounder of the Nicene Faith (Bp. Bull) does indeed speak very decidedly of Tertullian as a *lapser*, even when he wrote his first book against Marcion. His semi-schismatic position must be allowed. But, was it a *formal* lapse at that time? The English non-jurors were long in communion with the Church, even while they denounced their brethren and the "Erastianizing" clergy, much as Tertullian does the *Psychics*. St. Augustine speaks of *Tertullianists* with great moderation, and notes the final downfall of our author as something distinct from Tertullianism. When we reflect, therefore, that only four of all his varied writings (now extant) are proofs of an accomplished lapse, ought we not carefully to maintain the distinction between the Montanistic Tertullian and Tertullian the Montanist? Bishop Bull, it seems to me would not object to this way of putting it, when we consider his own discrimination in the following weighty words. He says:

"A clear distinction must be made between those works which Tertullian, when already a Montanist, wrote specifically in defense of Montanism *against the church*, and those which he composed, as a Montanist indeed, yet *not in defense of Montanism against the church*, but rather, *in defense of the common doctrines of the church*—and of Montanus, in opposition to other heretics."

Now in arranging the works of this second class, *the Prescription* comes logically first, because, written in Orthodoxy, it forcibly upholds the Scriptural Rule of Faith, the Catholic touchstone of all professed verity. It is also a necessary Introduction to the great work against Marcion which I have placed next in order; giving it the precedence to which it is entitled in part on chronological ground, in part because of the general purity of its material with the exhibition it presents of the author's mental processes and of his very gradual decline from Truth.

Very fortunate were the Edinburgh Editors in securing for this work and some others, the valuable labors of Dr. Holmes, of whom I have elsewhere given some biographical particulars. The merit and fullness of his annotations are so marked, that I have been spared a great deal of work, such as I was forced to bestow on the former volumes of this American Edition. But on the other hand these pages have given me much patient study and toil as an editor, because of the "shreds and patches" in which Tertullian comes to us, in the Edinburgh Series; and because of some typographical peculiarities, exceptional in that Series itself, and presenting complications, when transferred to a new form of mechanical arrangement.

For example, apart from some valuable material which belongs to the General Preface, and which I have transferred accordingly, the following dislocations confronted me to begin with: The *Marcion* is presented to us in Volume VII. apart from the other writings of Tertullian. At the close of Vol. XI. we reach the *Ad Nationes*, of which Dr. Holmes is the translator, another hand (Mr. Thelwall's) having been employed on former pages of that volume. It is not till we reach Volume XV. that Tertullian again appears, but this volume is wholly the work of Dr. Holmes. Finally, in Volume XVIII., we meet Tertullian again, (Mr. Thelwall the able translator), but, here is placed the "Introduction" to all the works of Tertullian, which, of course, I have, transferred to its proper place. I make these explanations by no means censoriously, but to point out at once the nature of my own task, and the advantage that accrues to the reader, by the order in which the works of the great Tertullian appear in this edition, enabling him to compare different or parallel passages, all methodically arranged in consecutive pages, without a minute's search, or delay.

Now, as to typographical difficulties to which I have referred, Dr. Holmes marks all his multiplied and useful notes with *brackets*, which are almost always superfluous, and which in this American Edition are used to designate my own contributions, when printed with the text, or apart from Preface and Elucidations. These, therefore, I have removed necessarily and with no appreciable loss to the work, but great gain to the beauty of the page. But, again, Dr. Holmes' translations are all so heavily bracketed as to become an eyesore, and the disfigured pages have been often complained of as afflictive to the reader. Many words strictly implied by the original Latin, and which should therefore be unmarked, are yet put between brackets. Even minute words (*and*, or *to wit*, or *again*,) when, in the nature of the case the English idiom requires them, are thus marked. I have not retained these blemishes; but when an inconsiderable word or a repetition does add to the sense, or qualify it, I have italicized such words, throwing more important interpolations into parenthetical marks, which are less painful to the sight than brackets. I have found them quite as serviceable to denote the auxiliary word or phrase; and where the author himself uses a parenthesis, I have observed very few instances in which a sensible reader would confound it with the translator's efforts to eke out the sense. Sometimes, an awkward interpolation has been thrown into a footnote.

Occasionally the crabbed sentences of the great Carthaginian are so obscure that Dr. Holmes has been unable to make them lucid, although, with the original in hand, he probably felt a force in his own rendering which the mere English reader must fail to perceive. In a few such instances, noting the fact in the margin, I have tried to bring out the sense, by slight modifications of punctuation and arrangement. Occasionally too I have dropped a superfluous interpolation (such as *e.g.*, *to conclude*, or let me say again,) when I have found that it only served to clog and overcharge a sentence. Last of all, Dr. Holmes' *headings* have sometimes been condensed, to avoid phrases and sentences immediately recurring in the chapter. These purely mechanical parts require a terse form of statement, like those in the English Bible, and I have frequently reduced them on that model, dropping redundant adverbs and adjectives to bring out the catchwords.

Against Praxeas

In Which He Defends, in all Essential Points, the Doctrine of the Holy Trinity.

Chapter I.—Satan's Wiles Against the Truth. How They Take the Form of the Praxean Heresy. Account of the Publication of This Heresy.

In various ways has the devil rivalled and resisted the truth. Sometimes his aim has been to destroy the truth by defending it. He maintains that there is one only Lord, the Almighty Creator of the world, in order that out of this doctrine of the unity he may fabricate a heresy. He says that the Father Himself came down into the Virgin, was Himself born of her, Himself suffered, indeed was Himself Jesus Christ. Here the old serpent has fallen out with himself, since, when he tempted Christ after John's baptism, he approached Him as "the Son of God;" surely intimating that God had a Son, even on the testimony of the very Scriptures, out of which he was at the moment forging his temptation: "If thou be the Son of God, command that these stones be made bread." Again: "If thou be the Son of God, cast thyself down from hence; for it is written, He shall give His angels charge concerning thee"—referring no doubt, to the Father— "and in their hands they shall bear thee up, that thou hurt not thy foot against a stone." Or perhaps, after all, he was only reproaching the Gospels with a lie, saying in fact: "Away with Matthew; away with Luke! Why heed their words? In spite of them, I declare that it was God Himself that I approached; it was the Almighty Himself that I tempted face to face; and it was for no other purpose than to tempt Him that I approached Him. If, on the contrary, it had been only the Son of God, most likely I should never have condescended to deal with Him." However, he is himself a liar from the beginning, and whatever man he instigates in his own way; as, for instance, Praxeas. For he was the first to import into Rome from Asia this kind of heretical pravity, a man in other respects of restless disposition, and above all inflated with the pride of confessorship simply and solely because he had to bear for a short time the annoyance of a prison; on which occasion, even "if he had given his body to be burned, it would have profited him nothing," not having the love of God, whose very gifts he has resisted and destroyed. For after the Bishop of Rome had acknowledged the prophetic gifts of Montanus, Prisca, and Maximilla, and, in consequence of the acknowledgment, had bestowed his peace on the churches of Asia and Phrygia, he, by importunately urging false accusations against the prophets themselves and their churches, and insisting on the authority of the bishop's predecessors in the see, compelled him to recall the pacific letter which he had issued, as well as to desist from his purpose of acknowledging the said gifts. By this Praxeas did a twofold service for the devil at Rome: he drove away prophecy, and he brought in heresy; he put to flight the Paraclete, and he crucified the Father. Praxeas' tares had been moreover sown, and had produced their fruit here also, while many were asleep in their simplicity of doctrine; but these tares actually seemed to have been plucked up, having been discovered and exposed by him whose agency God was pleased to employ. Indeed, Praxeas had deliberately resumed his old (true) faith, teaching it after his renunciation of error; and there is his own handwriting in evidence remaining among the carnally-minded, in whose society the transaction then took place; afterwards nothing was heard of him. We indeed, on our part, subsequently withdrew from the carnally-minded on our acknowledgment and maintenance of the Paraclete. But the tares of Praxeas had then everywhere shaken out their seed, which having lain hid for some while, with its vitality concealed under a mask, has now broken out with fresh life. But again shall it be rooted up, if the Lord will, even now; but if not now, in the day when all bundles of tares shall be gathered together, and along with every other stumbling-block shall be burnt up with unquenchable fire.

Chapter II. —The Catholic Doctrine of the Trinity and Unity, Sometimes Called the Divine Economy, or Dispensation of the Personal Relations of the Godhead.

In the course of time, then, the Father forsooth was born, and the Father suffered, God Himself, the Lord Almighty, whom in their preaching they declare to be Jesus Christ. We, however, as we indeed always have done (and more especially since we have been better instructed by the Paraclete, who leads men indeed into all truth), believe that there is one only God, but under the following dispensation, or οἰκονομία, as it is called, that this one only God has also a Son, His Word, who proceeded from Himself, by whom all things were made, and without whom nothing was made. Him we believe to have been sent by the Father into the Virgin, and to have been born of her—being both Man and God, the Son of Man and the Son of God, and to have been called by the name of Jesus Christ; we believe Him to have suffered, died, and been buried, according to the Scriptures, and, after He had been raised again by the Father and taken back to heaven, to be sitting at the right hand of the Father, and that He will come to judge the quick and the dead; who sent also from heaven from the Father, according to His own promise, the Holy Ghost, the Paraclete, the sanctifier of the faith of those who believe in the Father, and in the Son, and in the Holy Ghost. That this rule of faith has come down to us from the beginning of the gospel, even before any of the older heretics, much more before Praxeas, a pretender of yesterday, will be apparent both from the lateness of date which marks all heresies, and also from the absolutely novel character of our new-fangled Praxeas. In this principle also we must henceforth find a presumption of equal force against all heresies whatsoever—that whatever is first is true, whereas that is spurious which is later in date. But keeping this prescriptive rule inviolate, still some opportunity must be given for reviewing (the statements of heretics), with a view to the instruction and protection of divers persons; were it only that it may not seem that each perversion of the truth is condemned without examination, and simply prejudged; especially in the case of this heresy, which supposes itself to possess the pure truth, in thinking that one cannot believe in One Only God in any other way than by saying that the Father, the Son, and the Holy Ghost are the very selfsame Person. As if in this way also one were not All, in that All are of One, by unity (that is) of substance; while the mystery of the dispensation is still guarded, which distributes the Unity into a Trinity, placing in their order the three Persons—the Father, the Son, and the Holy Ghost: three, however, not in condition, but in degree; not in substance, but in form; not in power, but in aspect; yet of one substance, and of one condition, and of one power, inasmuch as He is one God, from whom these degrees and forms and aspects are reckoned, under the name of the Father, and of the Son, and of the Holy Ghost. How they are susceptible of number without division, will be shown as our treatise proceeds.

Chapter III. —Sundry Popular Fears and Prejudices. The Doctrine of the Trinity in Unity Rescued from These Misapprehensions.

The simple, indeed, (I will not call them unwise and unlearned,) who always constitute the majority of believers, are startled at the dispensation (of the Three in One), on the ground that their very rule of faith withdraws them from the world's plurality of gods to the one only true God; not understanding that, although He is the one only God, He must yet be believed in with His own οἰκονομία . The numerical order and distribution of the Trinity they assume to be a division of the Unity; whereas the Unity which derives the Trinity out of its own self is so far from being destroyed, that it is actually supported by it. They are constantly throwing out against us that we are preachers of two gods and three gods, while they take to themselves pre-eminently the credit of being worshippers of the One God; just as if the Unity itself with irrational deductions did not produce heresy, and the Trinity rationally considered constitute the truth. We, say they, maintain the Monarchy (or, sole government of God). And so, as far as the sound goes, do even Latins (and ignorant ones too) pronounce the word in such a way that you would suppose their understanding of the μοναρχία (or Monarchy) was as complete as their pronunciation of the term. Well, then Latins take pains to pronounce the μοναρχία(or Monarchy), while Greeks actually refuse to understand the οἰκονομία, or Dispensation (of the Three in One). As for myself, however, if I have gleaned any knowledge of either language, I am sure that μοναρχία(or Monarchy) has no other meaning than single and individual rule; but for all that, this monarchy does not, because it is the government of one, preclude him whose government it is, either from having a son, or from having made himself actually a son to himself, or from ministering his own monarchy by whatever agents he will. Nay more, I contend that no dominion so belongs to one only, as his own, or is in such a sense singular, or is in such a sense a monarchy, as not also to be administered through other persons most closely connected with it, and whom it has itself provided as officials to itself. If, moreover, there be a son belonging to him whose monarchy it is, it does not forthwith become divided and cease to be a monarchy, if the son also be taken as a sharer in it; but it is as to its origin equally his, by whom it is communicated to the son; and being his, it is quite as much a monarchy (or sole empire), since it is held together by two who are so inseparable. Therefore, inasmuch as the Divine Monarchy also is administered by so many legions and hosts of angels, according as it is written, “Thousand thousands ministered unto Him, and ten thousand times ten thousand stood before Him;” and since it has not from this circumstance ceased to be the rule of one (so as no longer to be a monarchy), because it is administered by so many thousands of powers; how comes it to pass that God should be thought to suffer division and severance in the

Son and in the Holy Ghost, who have the second and the third places assigned to them, and who are so closely joined with the Father in His substance, when He suffers no such (division and severance) in the multitude of so many angels? Do you really suppose that Those, who are naturally members of the Father's own substance, pledges of His love, instruments of His might, nay, His power itself and the entire system of His monarchy, are the overthrow and destruction thereof? You are not right in so thinking. I prefer your exercising yourself on the meaning of the thing rather than on the sound of the word. Now you must understand the overthrow of a monarchy to be this, when another dominion, which has a framework and a state peculiar to itself (and is therefore a rival), is brought in over and above it: when, e.g., some other god is introduced in opposition to the Creator, as in the opinions of Marcion; or when many gods are introduced, according to your Valentinuses and your Prodicuses. Then it amounts to an overthrow of the Monarchy, since it involves the destruction of the Creator.

Chapter IV. —The Unity of the Godhead and the Supremacy and Sole Government of the Divine Being. The Monarchy Not at All Impaired by the Catholic Doctrine.

But as for me, who derive the Son from no other source but from the substance of the Father, and (represent Him) as doing nothing without the Father's will, and as having received all power from the Father, how can I be possibly destroying the Monarchy from the faith, when I preserve it in the Son just as it was committed to Him by the Father? The same remark (I wish also to be formally) made by me with respect to the third degree in the Godhead, because I believe the Spirit to proceed from no other source than from the Father through the Son. Look to it then, that it be not you rather who are destroying the Monarchy, when you overthrow the arrangement and dispensation of it, which has been constituted in just as many names as it has pleased God to employ. But it remains so firm and stable in its own state, notwithstanding the introduction into it of the Trinity, that the Son actually has to restore it entire to the Father; even as the apostle says in his epistle, concerning the very end of all: "When He shall have delivered up the kingdom to God, even the Father; for He must reign till He hath put all enemies under His feet;" following of course the words of the Psalm: "Sit Thou on my right hand, until I make Thine enemies Thy footstool." "When, however, all things shall be subdued to Him, (with the exception of Him who did put all things under Him,) then shall the Son also Himself be subject unto Him who put all things under Him, that God may be all in all." We thus see that the Son is no obstacle to the Monarchy, although it is now administered by the Son; because with the Son it is still in its own state, and with its own state will be restored to the Father by the Son. No one, therefore, will impair it, on account of admitting the Son (to it), since it is certain that it has been committed to Him by the Father, and by and by has to be again delivered up by Him to the Father. Now, from this one passage of the epistle of the inspired apostle, we have been already able to show that the Father and the Son are two separate Persons, not only by the mention of their separate names as Father and the Son, but also by the fact that He who delivered up the kingdom, and He to whom it is delivered up—and in like manner, He who subjected (all things), and He to whom they were subjected—must necessarily be two different Beings.

Chapter V.—The Evolution of the Son or Word of God from the Father by a Divine Procession. Illustrated by the Operation of the Human Thought and Consciousness.

But since they will have the Two to be but One, so that the Father shall be deemed to be the same as the Son, it is only right that the whole question respecting the Son should be examined, as to whether He exists, and who He is and the mode of His existence. Thus shall the truth itself secure its own sanction from the Scriptures, and the interpretations which guard them. There are some who allege that even Genesis opens thus in Hebrew: "In the beginning God made for Himself a Son." As there is no ground for this, I am led to other arguments derived from God's own dispensation, in which He existed before the creation of the world, up to the generation of the Son. For before all things God was alone—being in Himself and for Himself universe, and space, and all things. Moreover, He was alone, because there was nothing external to Him but Himself. Yet even not then was He alone; for He had with Him that which He possessed in Himself, that is to say, His own Reason. For God is rational, and Reason was first in Him; and so all things were from Himself. This Reason is His own Thought (or Consciousness) which the Greeks call λόγος, by which term we also designate Word or Discourse and therefore it is now usual with our people, owing to the mere simple interpretation of the term, to say that the Word was in the beginning with God; although it would be more suitable to regard Reason as the more ancient; because God had not Word from the beginning, but He had Reason even before the beginning; because also Word itself consists of Reason, which it thus proves to have been the prior existence as being its own substance. Not that this distinction is of any practical moment. For although God had not yet sent out His Word, He still had Him within Himself, both in company with and included within His very Reason, as He silently planned and arranged within Himself everything which He was afterwards about to utter through His Word. Now, whilst He was thus planning and arranging with His own Reason, He was actually causing that to become Word which He was dealing with in the way of Word or Discourse. And that you may the more readily understand this, consider first of all, from your own self, who are made "in the image and likeness of God," for what purpose it is that you also possess reason in yourself, who are a rational creature, as being not only made by a rational Artificer, but actually animated out of His substance. Observe, then, that when you are silently conversing with yourself, this very process is carried on within you by your reason, which meets you with a word at every movement of your thought, at every impulse of your conception. Whatever you think, there is a word; whatever you conceive, there is reason. You must need speak it in your mind; and while you are speaking, you admit speech as an interlocutor with you, involved in which there is this very reason, whereby, while in thought you are holding converse with your word, you are (by reciprocal action) producing thought by means of that converse with your word. Thus, in a certain sense, the word is a second person within you, through which in thinking you utter speech, and through which also, (by reciprocity of process,) in uttering speech you generate thought. The word is itself a different thing from yourself. Now how much more fully is all this transacted in God, whose image and likeness even you are regarded as being, inasmuch as He has reason within Himself even while He is silent, and involved in that Reason His Word! I may therefore without rashness first lay this down (as a fixed principle) that even then before the creation of the universe God was not alone, since He had within Himself both Reason, and, inherent in Reason, His Word, which He made second to Himself by agitating it within Himself.

Chapter VI. —The Word of God is Also the Wisdom of God. The Going Forth of Wisdom to Create the Universe, According to the Divine Plan.

This power and disposition of the Divine Intelligence is set forth also in the Scriptures under the name of Σοφία, Wisdom; for what can be better entitled to the name of Wisdom than the Reason or the Word of God? Listen therefore to Wisdom herself, constituted in the character of a Second Person: “At the first the Lord created me as the beginning of His ways, with a view to His own works, before He made the earth, before the mountains were settled; moreover, before all the hills did He beget me;" that is to say, He created and generated me in His own intelligence. Then, again, observe the distinction between them implied in the companionship of Wisdom with the Lord. "When He prepared the heaven," says Wisdom, "I was present with Him; and when He made His strong places upon the winds, which are the clouds above; and when He secured the fountains, (and all things) which are beneath the sky, I was by, arranging all things with Him; I was by, in whom He delighted; and daily, too, did I rejoice in His presence." Now, as soon as it pleased God to put forth into their respective substances and forms the things which He had planned and ordered within Himself, in conjunction with His Wisdom's Reason and Word, He first put forth the Word Himself, having within Him His own inseparable Reason and Wisdom, in order that all things might be made through Him through whom they had been planned and disposed, yea, and already made, so far forth as (they were) in the mind and intelligence of God. This, however, was still wanting to them, that they should also be openly known, and kept permanently in their proper forms and substances.

Chapter VII. —The Son by Being Designated Word and Wisdom, (According to the Imperfection of Human Thought and Language) Liable to Be Deemed a Mere Attribute. He is Shown to Be a Personal Being.

Then, therefore, does the Word also Himself assume His own form and glorious garb, His own sound and vocal utterance, when God says, "Let there be light." This is the perfect nativity of the Word, when He proceeds forth from God—formed by Him first to devise and think out all things under the name of Wisdom— "The Lord created or formed me as the beginning of His ways;" then afterward begotten, to carry all into effect— "When He prepared the heaven, I was present with Him." Thus does He make Him equal to Him: for by proceeding from Himself He became His first-begotten Son, because begotten before all things; and His only-begotten also, because alone begotten of God, in a way peculiar to Himself, from the womb of His own heart—even as the Father Himself testifies: "My heart," says He, "hath emitted my most excellent Word." The Father took pleasure evermore in Him, who equally rejoiced with a reciprocal gladness in the Father's presence: "Thou art my Son, to-day have I begotten Thee;" even before the morning star did I beget Thee. The Son likewise acknowledges the Father, speaking in His own person, under the name of Wisdom: "The Lord formed Me as the beginning of His ways, with a view to His own works; before all the hills did He beget Me." For if indeed Wisdom in this passage seems to say that She was created by the Lord with a view to His works, and to accomplish His ways, yet proof is given in another Scripture that "all things were made by the Word, and without Him was there nothing made;" as, again, in another place (it is said), "By His word were the heavens established, and all the powers thereof by His Spirit"—that is to say, by the Spirit (or Divine Nature) which was in the Word: thus is it evident that it is one and the same power which is in one place described under the name of Wisdom, and in another passage under the appellation of the Word, which was initiated for the works of God which "strengthened the heavens;" "by which all things were made," "and without which nothing was made." Nor need we dwell any longer on this point, as if it were not the very Word Himself, who is spoken of under the name both of Wisdom and of Reason, and of the entire Divine Soul and Spirit. He became also the Son of God, and was begotten when He proceeded forth from Him. Do you then, (you ask,) grant that the Word is a certain substance, constructed by the Spirit and the communication of Wisdom? Certainly I do. But you will not allow Him to be really a substantive being, by having a substance of His own; in such a way that He may be regarded as an objective thing and a person, and so be able (as being constituted second to God the Father,) to make two, the Father and the Son, God and the

Word. For you will say, what is a word, but a voice and sound of the mouth, and (as the grammarians teach) air when struck against, intelligible to the ear, but for the rest a sort of void, empty, and incorporeal thing. I, on the contrary, contend that nothing empty and void could have come forth from God, seeing that it is not put forth from that which is empty and void; nor could that possibly be devoid of substance which has proceeded from so great a substance, and has produced such mighty substances: for all things which were made through Him, He Himself (personally) made. How could it be, that He Himself is nothing, without whom nothing was made? How could He who is empty have made things which are solid, and He who is void have made things which are full, and He who is incorporeal have made things which have body? For although a thing may sometimes be made different from him by whom it is made, yet nothing can be made by that which is a void and empty thing. Is that Word of God, then, a void and empty thing, which is called the Son, who Himself is designated God? "The Word was with God, and the Word was God." It is written, "Thou shalt not take God's name in vain." This for certain is He "who, being in the form of God, thought it not robbery to be equal with God." In what form of God? Of course he means in some form, not in none. For who will deny that God is a body, although "God is a Spirit?" For Spirit has a bodily substance of its own kind, in its own form. Now, even if invisible things, whatsoever they be, have both their substance and their form in God, whereby they are visible to God alone, how much more shall that which has been sent forth from His substance not be without substance! Whatever, therefore, was the substance of the Word that I designate a Person, I claim for it the name of Son; and while I recognize the Son, I assert His distinction as second to the Father.

Chapter VIII. —Though the Son or Word of God Emanates from the Father, He is Not, Like the Emanations of Valentinus, Separable from the Father. Nor is the Holy Ghost Separable from Either. Illustrations from Nature.

If any man from this shall think that I am introducing some προβολή—that is to say, some prolation of one thing out of another, as Valentinus does when he sets forth Æon from Æon, one after another—then this is my first reply to you: Truth must not therefore refrain from the use of such a term, and its reality and meaning, because heresy also employs it. The fact is, heresy has rather taken it from Truth, in order to mold it into its own counterfeit. Was the Word of God put forth or not? Here take your stand with me, and flinch not. If He was put forth, then acknowledge that the true doctrine has a prolation; and never mind heresy, when in any point it mimics the truth. The question now is, in what sense each side uses a given thing and the word which expresses it. Valentinus divides and separates his prolations from their Author, and places them at so great a distance from Him, that the Æon does not know the Father: he longs, indeed, to know Him, but cannot; nay, he is almost swallowed up and dissolved into the rest of matter. With us, however, the Son alone knows the Father, and has Himself unfolded "the Father's bosom." He has also heard and seen all things with the Father; and what He has been commanded by the Father, that also does He speak. And it is not His own will, but the Father's, which He has accomplished, which He had known most intimately, even from the beginning. "For what man knoweth the things which be in God, but the Spirit which is in Him?" But the Word was formed by the Spirit, and (if I may so express myself) the Spirit is the body of the Word. The Word, therefore, is both always in the Father, as He says, "I am in the Father;" and is always with God, according to what is written, "And the Word was with God;" and never separate from the Father, or other than the Father, since "I and the Father are one." This will be the prolation, taught by the truth, the guardian of the Unity, wherein we declare that the Son is a prolation from the Father, without being separated from Him. For God sent forth the Word, as the Paraclete also declares, just as the root puts forth the tree, and the fountain the river, and the sun the ray. For these are προβολαί, or emanations, of the substances from which they proceed. I should not hesitate, indeed, to call the tree the son or offspring of the root, and the river of the fountain, and the ray of the sun; because every original source is a parent, and everything which issues from the origin is an offspring. Much more is (this true of) the Word of God, who has actually received as His own peculiar designation the name of Son. But still the tree is not severed from the root, nor the river from the fountain, nor the ray from the sun; nor, indeed, is the Word separated from God. Following, therefore, the form of these analogies, I confess that I call God and His Word—the Father and His Son—two. For the root and the tree are distinctly two things, but correlatively joined; the fountain and the river are also two forms, but indivisible; so likewise the sun and the ray are two forms, but coherent ones. Everything which proceeds from something else must needs be second to that from which it proceeds, without being on that account separated. Where, however, there is a second, there must be two; and where there is a third, there must be three. Now the Spirit indeed is third from God and the Son; just as the fruit of the tree is third from the root, or as the stream out of the river is third from the fountain, or as the apex of the ray is third from the sun. Nothing, however, is alien from that original source whence it derives its own properties. In like manner the Trinity, flowing down from the Father through intertwined and connected steps, does not at all disturb the Monarchy, whilst it at the same time guards the state of the Economy.

Chapter IX. —The Catholic Rule of Faith Expounded in Some of Its Points. Especially in the Unconfused Distinction of the Several Persons of the Blessed Trinity.

Bear always in mind that this is the rule of faith which I profess; by it I testify that the Father, and the Son, and the Spirit are inseparable from each other, and so will you know in what sense this is said. Now, observe, my assertion is that the Father is one, and the Son one, and the Spirit one, and that They are distinct from Each Other. This statement is taken in a wrong sense by every uneducated as well as every perversely disposed person, as if it predicated a diversity, in such a sense as to imply a separation among the Father, and the Son, and the Spirit. I am, moreover, obliged to say this, when (extolling the Monarchy at the expense of the Economy) they contend for the identity of the Father and Son and Spirit, that it is not by way of diversity that the Son differs from the Father, but by distribution: it is not by division that He is different, but by distinction; because the Father is not the same as the Son, since they differ one from the other in the mode of their being. For the Father is the entire substance, but the Son is a derivation and portion of the whole, as He Himself acknowledges: "My Father is greater than I." In the Psalm His inferiority is described as being "a little lower than the angels." Thus the Father is distinct from the Son, being greater than the Son, inasmuch as He who begets is one, and He who is begotten is another; He, too, who sends is one, and He who is sent is another; and He, again, who makes is one, and He through whom the thing is made is another. Happily the Lord Himself employs this expression of the person of the Paraclete, so as to signify not a division or severance, but a disposition (of mutual relations in the Godhead); for He says, "I will pray the Father, and He shall send you another Comforter...even the Spirit of truth," thus making the Paraclete distinct from Himself, even as we say that the Son is also distinct from the Father; so that He showed a third degree in the Paraclete, as we believe the second degree is in the Son, by reason of the order observed in the Economy. Besides, does not the very fact that they have the distinct names of Father and Son amount to a declaration that they are distinct in personality? For, of course, all things will be what their names represent them to be; and what they are and ever will be, that will they be called; and the distinction indicated by the names does not at all admit of any confusion, because there is none in the things which they designate. "Yes is yes, and no is no; for what is more than these, cometh of evil."

Chapter X.—The Very Names of Father and Son Prove the Personal Distinction of the Two. They Cannot Possibly Be Identical, Nor is Their Identity Necessary to Preserve the Divine Monarchy.

So it is either the Father or the Son, and the day is not the same as the night; nor is the Father the same as the Son, in such a way that Both of them should be One, and One or the Other should be Both, —an opinion which the most conceited "Monarchians" maintain. He Himself, they say, made Himself a Son to Himself. Now a Father makes a Son, and a Son makes a Father; and they who thus become reciprocally related out of each other to each other cannot in any way by themselves simply become so related to themselves, that the Father can make Himself a Son to Himself, and the Son render Himself a Father to Himself. And the relations which God establishes, them does He also guard. A father must needs have a son, in order to be a father; so likewise a son, to be a son, must have a father. It is, however, one thing to have, and another thing to be. For instance, in order to be a husband, I must have a wife; I can never myself be my own wife. In like manner, in order to be a father, I have a son, for I never can be a son to myself; and in order to be a son, I have a father, it being impossible for me ever to be my own father. And it is these relations which make me (what I am), when I come to possess them: I shall then be a father, when I have a son; and a son, when I have a father. Now, if I am to be to myself any one of these relations, I no longer have what I am myself to be: neither a father, because I am to be my own father; nor a son, because I shall be my own son. Moreover, inasmuch as I ought to have one of these relations in order to be the other; so, if I am to be both together, I shall fail to be one while I possess not the other. For if I must be myself my son, who am also a father, I now cease to have a son, since I am my own son. But by reason of not having a son, since I am my own son, how can I be a father? For I ought to have a son, in order to be a father. Therefore, I am not a son, because I have not a father, who makes a son. In like manner, if I am myself my father, who am also a son, I no longer have a father, but am myself my father. By not having a father, however, since I am my own father, how can I be a son? For I ought to have a father, in order to be a son. I cannot therefore be a father, because I have not a son, who makes a father. Now all this must be the device of the devil—this excluding and severing one from the other—since by including both together in one under pretense of the Monarchy, he causes neither to be held and acknowledged, so that He is not the Father, since indeed He has not the Son; neither is He the Son, since in like manner He has not the Father: for while He is the Father, He will not be the Son. In this way they hold the Monarchy, but they hold neither the Father nor the Son. Well, but "with God nothing is impossible." True enough; who can be ignorant of it? Who also can be unaware that "the things which are impossible with men are possible with God?" "The foolish things also of the world hath God chosen to confound the things which are wise." We have read it all. Therefore, they argue, it was not difficult for God to make Himself both a Father and a Son, contrary to the condition of things among men. For a barren woman to have a child against nature was no difficulty with God; nor was it for a virgin to conceive. Of course nothing is "too hard for the Lord." But if we choose to apply this principle so extravagantly and harshly in our capricious imaginations, we may then make out God to have done anything we please, on the ground that it was not impossible for Him to do it. We must not, however, because He is able to do all things suppose that He has actually done what He has not done. But we must inquire whether He has really done it. God could, if He had liked, have furnished man with wings to fly with, just as He gave wings to kites. We must not, however, run to the conclusion that He did this because He was able to do it. He might also have extinguished Praxeas and all other heretics at once; it does not follow, however, that He did, simply because He was able. For it was necessary that there should be both kites and heretics; it was necessary also that the Father should be crucified. In one sense there will be something difficult even for God—namely, that which He has not done—not because He could not, but because He would not, do it. For with God, to be willing is to be able, and to be unwilling is to be unable; all that He has willed, however, He has both been able to accomplish, and has displayed His ability. Since, therefore, if God had wished to make Himself a Son to Himself, He had it in His power to do so; and since, if He had it in His power, He effected His purpose, you will then make good your proof of His power and His will (to do even this) when you shall have proved to us that He actually did it.

Chapter XI. —The Identity of the Father and the Son, as Praxeas Held It, Shown to Be Full of Perplexity and Absurdity. Many Scriptures Quoted in Proof of the Distinction of the Divine Persons of the Trinity.

It will be your duty, however, to adduce your proofs out of the Scriptures as plainly as we do, when we prove that He made His Word a Son to Himself. For if He calls Him Son, and if the Son is none other than He who has proceeded from the Father Himself, and if the Word has proceeded from the Father Himself, He will then be the Son, and not Himself from whom He proceeded. For the Father Himself did not proceed from Himself. Now, you who say that the Father is the same as the Son, do really make the same Person both to have sent forth from Himself (and at the same time to have gone out from Himself as) that Being which is God. If it was possible for Him to have done this, He at all events did not do it. You must bring forth the proof which I require of you—one like my own; that is, (you must prove to me) that the Scriptures show the Son and the Father to be the same, just as on our side the Father and the Son are demonstrated to be distinct; I say distinct, but not separate: for as on my part I produce the words of God Himself, "My heart hath emitted my most excellent Word," so you in like manner ought to adduce in opposition to me some text where God has said, "My heart hath emitted Myself as my own most excellent Word," in such a sense that He is Himself both the Emitter and the Emitted, both He who sent forth and He who was sent forth, since He is both the Word and God. I bid you also observe, that on my side I advance the passage where the Father said to the Son, "Thou art my Son, this day have I begotten Thee." If you want me to believe Him to be both the Father and the Son, show me some other passage where it is declared, "The Lord said unto Himself, I am my own Son, to-day have I begotten myself;" or again, "Before the morning did I beget myself;" and likewise, "I the Lord possessed Myself the beginning of my ways for my own works; before all the hills, too, did I beget myself;" and whatever other passages are to the same effect. Why, moreover, could God the Lord of all things, have hesitated to speak thus of Himself, if the fact had been so? Was He afraid of not being believed, if He had in so many words declared Himself to be both the Father and the Son? Of one thing He was at any rate afraid—of lying. Of Himself, too, and of His own truth, was He afraid. Believing Him, therefore, to be the true God, I am sure that He declared nothing to exist in any other way than according to His own dispensation and arrangement, and that He had arranged nothing in any other way than according to His own declaration. On your side, however, you must make Him out to be a liar, and an impostor, and a tamperer with His word, if, when He was Himself a Son to Himself, He assigned the part of His Son to be played by another, when all the Scriptures attest the clear existence of, and distinction in (the Persons of) the Trinity, and indeed furnish us with our Rule of faith, that He who speaks, and He of whom He speaks, and to whom He speaks, cannot possibly seem to be One and the Same. So absurd and misleading a statement would be unworthy of God, that, when it was Himself to whom He was speaking, He speaks rather to another, and not to His very self. Hear, then, other utterances also of the Father concerning the Son by the mouth of Isaiah: "Behold my Son, whom I have chosen; my beloved, in whom I am well pleased: I will put my Spirit upon Him, and He shall bring forth judgment to the Gentiles." Hear also what He says to the Son: "Is it a great thing for Thee, that Thou shouldest be called my Son to raise up the tribes of Jacob, and to restore the dispersed of Israel? I have given Thee for a light to the Gentiles, that Thou mayest be their salvation to the end of the earth." Hear now also the Son's utterances respecting the Father: "The Spirit of the Lord is upon me, because He hath anointed me to preach the gospel unto men." He speaks of Himself likewise to the Father in the Psalm: "Forsake me not until I have declared the might of Thine arm to all the generation that is to come." Also to the same purport in another Psalm: "O Lord, how are they increased that trouble me!" But almost all the Psalms which prophesy of the person of Christ, represent the Son as conversing with the Father—that is, represent Christ (as speaking) to God. Observe also the Spirit speaking of the Father and the Son, in the character of a third Person: "The Lord said unto my Lord, Sit Thou on my right hand, until I make Thine enemies Thy footstool." Likewise, in the words of Isaiah: "Thus saith the Lord to the Lord mine Anointed." Likewise, in the same prophet, He says to the Father respecting the Son: "Lord, who hath believed our report, as if He were a root in a dry ground, who had no form nor comeliness." These are a few testimonies out of many; for we do not pretend to bring up all the passages of Scripture, because we have a tolerably large accumulation of them in the various heads of our subject, as we in our several chapters call them in as our witnesses in the fullness of their dignity and authority. Still, in these few quotations the distinction of Persons in the Trinity is clearly set forth. For there is the Spirit Himself who speaks, and the Father to whom He speaks, and the Son of whom He speaks. In the same manner, the other passages also establish each one of several Persons in His special character—addressed as they in some cases are to the Father or to the Son respecting the Son, in other cases to the Son or to the Father concerning the Father, and again in other instances to the (Holy) Spirit.and to whom is the arm of the Lord revealed? We brought a report concerning Him, as if He were a little child, as if He were a root in a dry ground, who had no form nor comeliness." These are a few testimonies out of many; for we do not pretend to bring up all the passages of Scripture, because we have a tolerably large accumulation of them in the various heads of our subject, as we in our several chapters call them in as our witnesses in the fullness of their dignity and authority. Still, in these few quotations the distinction of Persons in the Trinity is clearly set forth. For there is the Spirit Himself who speaks, and the Father to whom He speaks, and the Son of whom He speaks. In the same manner, the other passages also establish each one of several Persons in His special character—addressed as they in some cases are to the Father or to the Son respecting the Son, in other cases to the Son or to the Father concerning the Father, and again in other instances to the (Holy) Spirit.

Chapter XII. —Other Quotations from Holy Scripture Adduced in Proof of the Plurality of Persons in the Godhead.

If the number of the Trinity also offends you, as if it were not connected in the simple Unity, I ask you how it is possible for a Being who is merely and absolutely One and Singular, to speak in plural phrase, saying, "Let us make man in our own image, and after our own likeness;" whereas He ought to have said, "Let me make man in my own image, and after my own likeness," as being a unique and singular Being? In the following passage, however, "Behold the man is become as one of us," He is either deceiving or amusing us in speaking plurally, if He is One only and singular. Or was it to the angels that He spoke, as the Jews interpret the passage, because these also acknowledge not the Son? Or was it because He was at once the Father, the Son, and the Spirit, that He spoke to Himself in plural terms, making Himself plural on that very account? Nay, it was because He had already His Son close at His side, as a second Person, His own Word, and a third Person also, the Spirit in the Word, that He purposely adopted the plural phrase, "Let us make;" and, "in our image;" and, "become as one of us." For with whom did He make man? and to whom did He make him like? (The answer must be), the Son on the one hand, who was one day to put on human nature; and the Spirit on the other, who was to sanctify man. With these did He then speak, in the Unity of the Trinity, as with His ministers and witnesses. In the following text also He distinguishes among the Persons: "So God created man in His own image; in the image of God created He him." Why say "image of God?" Why not "His own image" merely, if He was only one who was the Maker, and if there was not also One in whose image He made man? But there was One in whose image God was making man, that is to say, Christ's image, who, being one day about to become Man (more surely and more truly so), had already caused the man to be called His image, who was then going to be formed of clay—the image and similitude of the true and perfect Man. But in respect of the previous works of the world what says the Scripture? Its first statement indeed is made, when the Son has not yet appeared: "And God said, Let there be light, and there was light." Immediately there appears the Word, "that true light, which lighteth man on his coming into the world," and through Him also came light upon the world. From that moment God willed creation to be effected in the Word, Christ being present and ministering unto Him: and so God created. And God said, "Let there be a firmament…and God made the firmament;" and God also said, "Let there be lights (in the firmament); and so God made a greater and a lesser light." But all the rest of the created things did He in like manner make, who made the former ones—I mean the Word of God, "through whom all things were made, and without whom nothing was made." Now if He too is God, according to John, (who says,) "The Word was God," then you have two Beings—One that commands that the thing be made, and the Other that executes the order and creates. In what sense, however, you ought to understand Him to be another, I have already explained, on the ground of Personality, not of Substance—in the way of distinction, not of division. But although I must everywhere hold one only substance in three coherent and inseparable (Persons), yet I am bound to acknowledge, from the necessity of the case, that He who issues a command is different from Him who executes it. For, indeed, He would not be issuing a command if He were all the while doing the work Himself, while ordering it to be done by the second. But still He did issue the command, although He would not have intended to command Himself if He were only one; or else He must have worked without any command, because He would not have waited to command Himself.

Chapter XIII. —The Force of Sundry Passages of Scripture Illustrated in Relation to the Plurality of Persons and Unity of Substance. There is No Polytheism Here, Since the Unity is Insisted on as a Remedy Against Polytheism.

Well then, you reply, if He was God who spoke, and He was also God who created, at this rate, one God spoke and another created; (and thus) two Gods are declared. If you are so venturesome and harsh, reflect a while; and that you may think the better and more deliberately, listen to the psalm in which Two are described as God: "Thy throne, O God, is for ever and ever; the scepter of Thy kingdom is a scepter of righteousness. Thou hast loved righteousness, and hated iniquity: therefore, God, even Thy God, hath anointed Thee or made Thee His Christ." Now, since He here speaks to God, and affirms that God is anointed by God, He must have affirmed that Two are God, by reason of the scepter's royal power. Accordingly, Isaiah also says to the Person of Christ: "The Sabæans, men of stature, shall pass over to Thee; and they shall follow after Thee, bound in fetters; and they shall worship Thee, because God is in Thee: for Thou art our God, yet we knew it not; Thou art the God of Israel." For here too, by saying, "God is in Thee," and "Thou art God," he sets forth Two who were God: (in the former expression in Thee, he means) in Christ, and (in the other he means) the Holy Ghost. That is a still grander statement which you will find expressly made in the Gospel: "In the beginning was the Word, and the Word was with God, and the Word was God." There was One "who was," and there was another "with whom" He was. But I find in Scripture the name Lord also applied to them Both: "The Lord said unto my Lord, Sit Thou on my right hand." And Isaiah says this: "Lord, who hath believed our report, and to whom is the arm of the Lord revealed?" Now he would most certainly have said Thine Arm, if he had not wished us to understand that the Father is Lord, and the Son also is Lord. A much more ancient testimony we have also in Genesis: "Then the Lord rained upon Sodom and upon Gomorrah brimstone and fire from the Lord out of heaven." Now, either deny that this is Scripture; or else (let me ask) what sort of man you are, that you do not think words ought to be taken and understood in the sense in which they are written, especially when they are not expressed in allegories and parables, but in determinate and simple declarations? If, indeed, you follow those who did not at the time endure the Lord when showing Himself to be the Son of God, because they would not believe Him to be the Lord, then (I ask you) call to mind along with them the passage where it is written, "I have said, Ye are gods, and ye are children of the Most High;" and again, "God standeth in the congregation of gods;" in order that, if the Scripture has not been afraid to designate as gods human beings, who have become sons of God by faith, you may be sure that the same Scripture has with greater propriety conferred the name of the Lord on the true and one only Son of God. Very well! you say, I shall challenge you to preach from this day forth (and that, too, on the authority of these same Scriptures) two Gods and two Lords, consistently with your views. God forbid, (is my reply). For we, who by the grace of God possess an insight into both the times and the occasions of the Sacred Writings, especially we who are followers of the Paraclete, not of human teachers, do indeed definitively declare that Two Beings are God, the Father and the Son, and, with the addition of the Holy Spirit, even Three, according to the principle of the divine economy, which introduces number, in order that the Father may not, as you perversely infer, be Himself believed to have been born and to have suffered, which it is not lawful to believe, forasmuch as it has not been so handed down. That there are, however, two Gods or two Lords, is a statement which at no time proceeds out of our mouth: not as if it were untrue that the Father is God, and the Son is God, and the Holy Ghost is God, and each is God; but because in earlier times Two were actually spoken of as God, and two as Lord, that when Christ should come He might be both acknowledged as God and designated as Lord, being the Son of Him who is both God and Lord. Now, if there were found in the Scriptures but one Personality of Him who is God and Lord, Christ would justly enough be inadmissible to the title of God and Lord: for (in the Scriptures) there was declared to be none other than One God and One Lord, and it must have followed that the Father should Himself seem to have come down (to earth), inasmuch as only One God and One Lord was ever read of (in the Scriptures), and His entire Economy would be involved in obscurity, which has been planned and arranged with so clear a foresight in His providential dispensation as matter for our faith. As soon, however, as Christ came, and was recognized by us as the very Being who had from the beginning caused plurality (in the Divine Economy), being the second from the Father, and with the Spirit the third, and Himself declaring and manifesting the Father more fully (than He had ever been before), the title of Him who is God and Lord was at once restored to the Unity (of the Divine Nature), even because the Gentiles would have to pass from the multitude of their idols to the One Only God, in order that a difference might be distinctly settled between the worshippers of One God and the votaries of polytheism. For it was only right that Christians should shine in the world as "children of light," adoring and invoking Him who is the One God and Lord as "the light of the world." Besides, if, from that perfect knowledge which assures us that the title of God and Lord is suitable both to the Father, and to the Son, and to the Holy Ghost, we were to invoke a plurality of gods and lords, we should quench our torches, and we should become less courageous to endure the martyr's sufferings, from which an easy escape would everywhere lie open to us, as soon as we swore by a plurality of gods and lords, as sundry heretics do, who hold more gods than One. I will therefore not speak of gods at all, nor of lords, but I shall follow the apostle; so that if the Father and the Son, are alike to be invoked, I shall call the Father "God," and invoke Jesus Christ as "Lord." But when Christ alone (is mentioned), I shall be able to call Him "God," as the same apostle says: "Of whom is Christ, who is over all, God blessed forever." For I should give the name of "sun" even to a sunbeam, considered in itself; but if I were mentioning the sun from which the ray emanates, I certainly should at once withdraw the name of sun from the mere beam. For although I make not two suns, still I shall reckon both the sun and its ray to be as much two things and two forms of one undivided substance, as God and His Word, as the Father and the Son.

Chapter XIV. —The Natural Invisibility of the Father, and the Visibility of the Son Witnessed in Many Passages of the Old Testament. Arguments of Their Distinctness, Thus Supplied.

Moreover, there comes to our aid, when we insist upon the Father and the Son as being Two, that regulating principle which has determined God to be invisible. When Moses in Egypt desired to see the face of the Lord, saying, "If therefore I have found grace in Thy sight, manifest Thyself unto me, that I may see Thee and know Thee," God said, "Thou canst not see my face; for there shall no man see me, and live:" in other words, he who sees me shall die. Now we find that God has been seen by many persons, and yet that no one who saw Him died (at the sight). The truth is, they saw God according to the faculties of men, but not in accordance with the full glory of the Godhead. For the patriarchs are said to have seen God (as Abraham and Jacob), and the prophets (as, for instance Isaiah and Ezekiel), and yet they did not die. Either, then, they ought to have died, since they had seen Him—for (the sentence runs), "No man shall see God, and live;" or else if they saw God, and yet did not die, the Scripture is false in stating that God said, "If a man see my face, he shall not live." Either way, the Scripture misleads us, when it makes God invisible, and when it produces Him to our sight. Now, then, He must be a different Being who was seen, because of one who was seen it could not be predicated that He is invisible. It will therefore follow, that by Him who is invisible we must understand the Father in the fullness of His majesty, while we recognize the Son as visible by reason of the dispensation of His derived existence; even as it is not permitted us to contemplate the sun, in the full amount of his substance which is in the heavens, but we can only endure with our eyes a ray, by reason of the tempered condition of this portion which is projected from him to the earth. Here someone on the other side may be disposed to contend that the Son is also invisible as being the Word, and as being also the

Spirit; and, while claiming one nature for the Father and the Son, to affirm that the Father is rather One and the Same Person with the Son. But the Scripture, as we have said, maintains their difference by the distinction it makes between the Visible and the Invisible. They then go on to argue to this effect, that if it was the Son who then spoke to Moses, He must mean it of Himself that His face was visible to no one, because He was Himself indeed the invisible Father in the name of the Son. And by this means they will have it that the Visible and the Invisible are one and the same, just as the Father and the Son are the same; (and this they maintain) because in a preceding passage, before He had refused (the sight of) His face to Moses, the Scripture informs us that "the Lord spoke face to face with Moses, even as a man speaketh unto his friend;" just as Jacob also says, "I have seen God face to face." Therefore, the Visible and the Invisible are one and the same; and both being thus the same, it follows that He is invisible as the Father, and visible as the Son. As if the Scripture, according to our exposition of it, were inapplicable to the Son, when the Father is set aside in His own invisibility. We declare, however, that the Son also, considered in Himself (as the Son), is invisible, in that He is God, and the Word and Spirit of God; but that He was visible before the days of His flesh, in the way that He says to Aaron and Miriam, "And if there shall be a prophet amongst you, I will make myself known to him in a vision, and will speak to him in a dream; not as with Moses, with whom I shall speak mouth to mouth, even apparently, that is to say, in truth, and not enigmatically," that is to say, in image; as the apostle also expresses it, "Now we see through a glass, darkly (or enigmatically), but then face to face." Since, therefore, He reserves to some future time His presence and speech face to face with Moses—a promise which was afterwards fulfilled in the retirement of the mount (of transfiguration), when as we read in the Gospel, "Moses appeared talking with Jesus"—it is evident that in early times it was always in a glass, (as it were,) and an enigma, in vision and dream, that God, I mean the Son of God, appeared—to the prophets and the patriarchs, as also to Moses indeed himself. And even if the Lord did possibly speak with him face to face, yet it was not as man that he could behold His face, unless indeed it was in a glass, (as it were,) and by enigma. Besides, if the Lord so spoke with Moses, that Moses actually discerned His face, eye to eye, how comes it to pass that immediately afterwards, on the same occasion, he desires to see His face, which he ought not to have desired, because he had already seen it? And how, in like manner, does the Lord also say that His face cannot be seen, because He had shown it, if indeed He really had, (as our opponents suppose). Or what is that face of God, the sight of which is refused, if there was one which was visible to man? "I have seen God," says Jacob, "face to face, and my life is preserved." There ought to be some other face which kills if it be only seen. Well, then, was the Son visible? (Certainly not,) although He was the face of God, except only in vision and dream, and in a glass and enigma, because the Word and Spirit (of God) cannot be seen except in an imaginary form. But, (they say,) He calls the invisible Father His face. For who is the Father? Must He not be the face of the Son, by reason of that authority which He obtains as the begotten of the Father? For is there not a natural propriety in saying of some personage greater (than yourself), That man is my face; he gives me his countenance? "My Father," says Christ, "is greater than I." Therefore, the Father must be the face of the Son. For what does the Scripture say? "The Spirit of His person is Christ the Lord." As therefore Christ is the Spirit of the Father's person, there is good reason why, in virtue indeed of the unity, the Spirit of Him to whose person He belonged—that is to say, the Father—pronounced Him to be His "face." Now this, to be sure, is an astonishing thing, that the Father can be taken to be the face of the Son, when He is His head; for "the head of Christ is God."

Chapter XV. —New Testament Passages Quoted. They Attest the Same Truth of the Son's Visibility Contrasted with the Father's Invisibility.

If I fail in resolving this article (of our faith) by passages which may admit of dispute out of the Old Testament, I will take out of the New Testament a confirmation of our view, that you may not straightway attribute to the Father every possible (relation and condition) which I ascribe to the Son. Behold, then, I find both in the Gospels and in the (writings of the) apostles a visible and an invisible God (revealed to us), under a manifest and personal distinction in the condition of both. There is a certain emphatic saying by John: "No man hath seen God at any time;" meaning, of course, at any previous time. But he has indeed taken away all question of time, by saying that God had never been seen. The apostle confirms this statement; for, speaking of God, he says, "Whom no man hath seen, nor can see;" because the man indeed would die who should see Him. But the very same apostles testify that they had both seen and "handled" Christ. Now, if Christ is Himself both the Father and the Son, how can He be both the Visible and the Invisible? In order, however, to reconcile this diversity between the Visible and the Invisible, will not someone on the other side argue that the two statements are quite correct: that He was visible indeed in the flesh, but was invisible before His appearance in the flesh; so that He who as the Father was invisible before the flesh, is the same as the Son who was visible in the flesh? If, however, He is the same who was invisible before the incarnation, how comes it that He was actually seen in ancient times before (coming in) the flesh? And by parity of reasoning, if He is the same who was visible after (coming in) the flesh, how happens it that He is now declared to be invisible by the apostles? How, I repeat, can all this be, unless it be that He is one, who anciently was visible only in mystery and enigma, and became more clearly visible by His incarnation, even the Word who was also made flesh;

whilst He is another whom no man has seen at any time, being none else than the Father, even Him to whom the Word belongs? Let us, in short, examine who it is whom the apostles saw. "That," says John, "which we have seen with our eyes, which we have looked upon, and our hands have handled, of the Word of life." Now the Word of life became flesh, and was heard, and was seen, and was handled, because He was flesh who, before He came in the flesh, was the "Word in the beginning with God" the Father, and not the Father with the Word. For although the Word was God, yet was He with God, because He is God of God; and being joined to the Father, is with the Father. "And we have seen His glory, the glory as of the only begotten of the Father;" that is, of course, (the glory) of the Son, even Him who was visible, and was glorified by the invisible Father. And therefore, inasmuch as he had said that the Word of God was God, in order that he might give no help to the presumption of the adversary, (which pretended) that he had seen the Father Himself and in order to draw a distinction between the invisible Father and the visible Son, he makes the additional assertion, ex abundanti as it were: "No man hath seen God at any time." What God does he mean? The Word? But he has already said: "Him we have seen and heard, and our hands have handled the Word of life." Well, (I must again ask,) what God does he mean? It is of course the Father, with whom was the Word, the only begotten Son, who is in the bosom of the Father, and has Himself declared Him. He was both heard and seen and, that He might not be supposed to be a phantom, was actually handled. Him, too, did Paul behold; but yet he saw not the Father. "Have I not," he says, "seen Jesus Christ our Lord?" Moreover, he expressly called Christ God, saying: "Of whom are the fathers, and of whom as concerning the flesh Christ came, who is over all, God blessed forever." He shows us also that the Son of God, which is the Word of God, is visible, because He who became flesh was called Christ. Of the Father, however, he says to Timothy: "Whom none among men hath seen, nor indeed can see;" and he accumulates the description in still ampler terms: "Who only hath immortality, and dwelleth in the light which no man can approach unto." It was of Him, too, that he had said in a previous passage: "Now unto the King eternal, immortal, invisible, to the only God;" so that we might apply even the contrary qualities to the Son Himself—mortality, accessibility—of whom the apostle testifies that "He died according to the Scriptures," and that "He was seen by himself last of all,"—by means, of course, of the light which was accessible, although it was not without imperiling his sight that he experienced that light. A like danger to which also befell Peter, and John, and James, (who confronted not the same light) without risking the loss of their reason and mind; and if they, who were unable to endure the glory of the Son, had only seen the Father, they must have died then and there: "For no man shall see God, and live." This being the case, it is evident that He was always seen from the beginning, who became visible in the end; and that He, (on the contrary,) was not seen in the end who had never been visible from the beginning; and that accordingly there are two—the Visible and the Invisible. It was the Son, therefore, who was always seen, and the Son who always conversed with men, and the Son who has always worked by the authority and will of the Father; because "the Son can do nothing of Himself, but what He seeth the Father do"—"do" that is, in His mind and thought. For the Father acts by mind and thought; whilst the Son, who is in the Father's mind and thought, gives effect and form to what He sees. Thus all things were made by the Son, and without Him was not anything made.

Chapter XVI. —Early Manifestations of the Son of God, as Recorded in the Old Testament; Rehearsals of His Subsequent Incarnation.

But you must not suppose that only the works which relate to the (creation of the) world were made by the Son, but also whatsoever since that time has been done by God. For "the Father who loveth the Son, and hath given all things into His hand," loves Him indeed from the beginning, and from the very first has handed all things over to Him. Whence it is written, "From the beginning the Word was with God, and the Word was God;" to whom "is given by the Father all power in heaven and on earth." "The Father judgeth no man, but hath committed all judgment to the Son"—from the very beginning even. For when He speaks of all power and all judgment, and says that all things were made by Him, and all things have been delivered into His hand, He allows no exception (in respect) of time, because they would not be all things unless they were the things of all time. It is the Son, therefore, who has been from the beginning administering judgment, throwing down the haughty tower, and dividing the tongues, punishing the whole world by the violence of waters, raining upon Sodom and Gomorrah fire and brimstone, as the Lord from the Lord. For He it was who at all times came down to hold converse with men, from Adam on to the patriarchs and the prophets, in vision, in dream, in mirror, in dark saying; ever from the beginning laying the foundation of the course of His dispensations, which He meant to follow out to the very last. Thus was He ever learning even as God to converse with men upon earth, being no other than the Word which was to be made flesh. But He was thus learning (or rehearsing), in order to level for us the way of faith, that we might the more readily believe that the Son of God had come down into the world, if we knew that in times past also something similar had been done. For as it was on our account and for our learning that these events are described in the Scriptures, so for our sakes also were they done— (even ours, I say), "upon whom the ends of the world are come." In this way it was that even then He knew full well what human feelings and affections were, intending as He always did to take upon Him man's actual component substances, body and soul, making inquiry of Adam (as if He were ignorant), "Where art thou, Adam?"—repenting that He had made man, as if He had lacked foresight; tempting Abraham, as if ignorant of what was in man; offended with persons, and then reconciled to them; and whatever other (weaknesses and imperfections) the heretics lay hold of (in their assumptions) as unworthy of God, in order to discredit the Creator, not considering that these circumstances are suitable enough for the Son, who was one day to experience even human sufferings—hunger and thirst, and tears, and actual birth and real death, and in respect of such a dispensation "made by the Father a little less than the angels." But the heretics, you may be sure, will not allow that those things are suitable even to the Son of God, which you are imputing to the very Father Himself, when you pretend that He made Himself less (than the angels) on our account; whereas the Scripture informs us that He who was made less was so affected by another, and not Himself by Himself. What, again, if He was One who was "crowned with glory and honor," and He Another by whom He was so crowned, —the Son, in fact, by the Father? Moreover, how comes it to pass, that the Almighty Invisible God, "whom no man hath seen nor can see; He who dwelleth in light unapproachable;" "He who dwelleth not in temples made with hands;" "from before whose sight the earth trembles, and the mountains melt like wax;" who holdeth the whole world in His hand "like a nest;" "whose throne is heaven, and earth His footstool;" in whom is every place, but Himself is in no place; who is the utmost bound of the universe;—how happens it, I say, that He (who, though) the Most High, should yet have walked in paradise towards the cool of the evening, in quest of Adam; and should have shut up the ark after Noah had entered it; and at Abraham's tent should have refreshed Himself under an oak; and have called to Moses out of the burning bush; and have appeared as "the fourth" in the furnace of the Babylonian monarch (although He is there called the Son of man),—unless all these events had happened as an image, as a mirror, as an enigma (of the future incarnation)? Surely even these things could not have been

Hence, therefore, their error becomes manifest; for, being ignorant that the entire order of the divine administration has from the very first had its course through the agency of the Son, they believe that the Father Himself was actually seen, and held converse with men, and worked, and was athirst, and suffered hunger (in spite of the prophet who says: "The everlasting God, the Lord, the Creator of the ends of the earth, shall never thirst at all, nor be hungry;" much more, shall neither die at any time, nor be buried!), and therefore that it was uniformly one God, even the Father, who at all times did Himself the things which were really done by Him through the agency of the Son.believed even of the Son of God, unless they had been given us in the Scriptures; possibly also they could not have been believed of the Father, even if they had been given in the Scriptures, since these men bring Him down into Mary's womb, and set Him before Pilate's judgment-seat, and bury Him in the sepulcher of Joseph.

Chapter XVII. —Sundry August Titles, Descriptive of Deity, Applied to the Son, Not, as Praxeas Would Have It, Only to the Father.

They more readily supposed that the Father acted in the Son's name, than that the Son acted in the Father's; although the Lord says Himself, "I am come in my Father's name;" and even to the Father He declares, "I have manifested Thy name unto these men;" whilst the Scripture likewise says, "Blessed is He that cometh in the name of the Lord," that is to say, the Son in the Father's name. And as for the Father's names, God Almighty, the Most High, the Lord of hosts, the King of Israel, the "One that is," we say (for so much do the Scriptures teach us) that they belonged suitably to the Son also, and that the Son came under these designations, and has always acted in them, and has thus manifested them in Himself to men. "All things," says He, "which the Father hath are mine." Then why not His names also? When, therefore, you read of Almighty God, and the Most High, and the God of hosts, and the King of Israel, the "One that is," consider whether the Son also be not indicated by these designations, who in His own right is God Almighty, in that He is the Word of Almighty God, and has received power over all; is the Most High, in that He is "exalted at the right hand of God," as Peter declares in the Acts; is the Lord of hosts, because all things are by the Father made subject to Him; is the King of Israel because to Him has especially been committed the destiny of that nation; and is likewise "the One that is," because there are many who are called Sons, but are not. As to the point maintained by them, that the name of Christ belongs also to the Father, they shall hear (what I have to say) in the proper place. Meanwhile, let this be my immediate answer to the argument which they adduce from the Revelation of John: "I am the Lord which is, and which was, and which is to come, the Almighty;" and from all other passages which in their opinion make the designation of Almighty God unsuitable to the Son. As if, indeed, He which is to come were not almighty; whereas even the Son of the Almighty is as much almighty as the Son of God is God.

Chapter XVIII. —The Designation of the One God in the Prophetic Scriptures. Intended as a Protest Against Heathen Idolatry, It Does Not Preclude the Correlative Idea of the Son of God. The Son is in the Father.

But what hinders them from readily perceiving this community of the Father's titles in the Son, is the statement of Scripture, whenever it determines God to be but One; as if the selfsame Scripture had not also set forth Two both as God and Lord, as we have shown above. Their argument is: Since we find Two and One, therefore Both are One and the Same, both Father and Son. Now the Scripture is not in danger of requiring the aid of any one's argument, lest it should seem to be self-contradictory. It has a method of its own, both when it sets forth one only God, and also when it shows that there are

Two, Father and Son; and is consistent with itself. It is clear that the Son is mentioned by it. For, without any detriment to the Son, it is quite possible for it to have rightly determined that God is only One, to whom the Son belongs; since He who has a Son ceases not on that account to exist, —Himself being One only, that is, on His own account, whenever He is named without the Son. And He is named without the Son when so ever He is defined as the principle (of Deity) in the character of "its first Person," which had to be mentioned before the name of the Son; because it is the Father who is acknowledged in the first place, and after the Father the Son is named. Therefore "there is one God," the Father, "and without Him there is none else." And when He Himself makes this declaration, He denies not the Son, but says that there is no other God; and the Son is not different from the Father. Indeed, if you only look carefully at the contexts which follow such statements as this, you will find that they nearly always have distinct reference to the makers of idols and the worshippers thereof, with a view to the multitude of false gods being expelled by the unity of the Godhead, which nevertheless has a Son; and inasmuch as this Son is undivided and inseparable from the Father, so is He to be reckoned as being in the Father, even when He is not named. The fact is, if He had named Him expressly, He would have separated Him, saying in so many words: "Beside me there is none else, except my Son." In short He would have made His Son actually another, after excepting Him from others. Suppose the sun to say, "I am the Sun, and there is none other besides me, except my ray," would you not have remarked how useless was such a statement, as if the ray were not itself reckoned in the sun? He says, then, that there is no God besides Himself in respect of the idolatry both of the Gentiles as well as of Israel; nay, even on account of our heretics also, who fabricate idols with their words, just as the heathen do with their hands; that is to say, they make another God and another Christ. When, therefore, He attested His own unity, the Father took care of the Son's interests, that Christ should not be supposed to have come from another God, but from Him who had already said, "I am God and there is none other beside me," who shows us that He is the only God, but in company with His Son, with whom "He stretcheth out the heavens alone."

Chapter XIX. —The Son in Union with the Father in the Creation of All Things. This Union of the Two in Co-Operation is Not Opposed to the True Unity of God. It is Opposed Only to Praxeas' Identification Theory.

But this very declaration of His they will hastily pervert into an argument of His singleness. "I have," says He, "stretched out the heaven alone." Undoubtedly alone as regards all other powers; and He thus gives a premonitory evidence against the conjectures of the heretics, who maintain that the world was constructed by various angels and powers, who also make the Creator Himself to have been either an angel or some subordinate agent sent to form external things, such as the constituent parts of the world, but who was at the same time ignorant of the divine purpose. If, now, it is in this sense that He stretches out the heavens alone, how is it that these heretics assume their position so perversely, as to render inadmissible the singleness of that Wisdom which says, "When He prepared the heaven, I was present with Him?"—even though the apostle asks, "Who hath known the mind of the Lord, or who hath been His counsellor?" meaning, of course, to except that wisdom which was present with Him. In Him, at any rate, and with Him, did (Wisdom) construct the universe, He not being ignorant of what she was making. "Except Wisdom," however, is a phrase of the same sense exactly as "except the Son," who is Christ, "the Wisdom and Power of God," according to the apostle, who only knows the mind of the Father. "For who knoweth the things that be in God, except the Spirit which is in Him?" Not, observe, without Him. There was therefore One who caused God to be not alone, except "alone" from all other gods. But (if we are to follow the heretics), the Gospel itself will have to be rejected, because it tells us that all things were made by God through the Word, without whom nothing was made. And if I am not mistaken, there is also another passage in which it is written: "By the Word of the Lord were the heavens made, and all the hosts of them by His Spirit." Now this Word, the Power of God and the Wisdom of God, must be the very Son of God. So that, if (He did) all things by the Son, He must have stretched out the heavens by the Son, and so not have stretched them out alone, except in the sense in which He is "alone" (and apart) from all other gods. Accordingly, He says, concerning the Son, immediately afterwards: "Who else is it that frustrateth the tokens of the liars, and maketh diviners mad, turning wise men backward, and making their knowledge foolish, and confirming the words of His Son?"—as, for instance, when He said, "This is my beloved Son, in whom I am well pleased; hear ye Him." By thus attaching the Son to Himself, He becomes His own interpreter in what sense He stretched out the heavens alone, meaning alone with His Son, even as He is one with His Son. The utterance, therefore, will be in like manner the Son's, "I have stretched out the heavens alone," because by the Word were the heavens established. Inasmuch, then, as the heaven was prepared when Wisdom was present in the Word, and since all things were made by the Word, it is quite correct to say that even the Son stretched out the heaven alone, because He alone ministered to the Father's work. It must also be He who says, "I am the First, and to all futurity I AM." The Word, no doubt, was before all things. "In the beginning was the Word;" and in that beginning He was sent forth by the Father. The Father, however, has no beginning, as proceeding from none; nor can He be seen, since He was not begotten. He who has always been alone could never have had order or rank. Therefore, if they have determined that the Father and the Son must be regarded as one and the same, for the express purpose of vindicating the unity of God, that unity of His is preserved intact; for He is one, and yet He has a Son, who is equally with Himself comprehended in the same Scriptures. Since they are unwilling to allow that the Son is a distinct Person, second from the Father, lest, being thus second, He should cause two Gods to be spoken of, we have shown above that Two are actually described in Scripture as God and Lord. And to prevent their being offended at this fact, we give a reason why they are not said to be two Gods and two Lords, but that they are two as Father and Son; and this not by severance of their substance, but from the dispensation wherein we declare the Son to be undivided and inseparable from the Father, —distinct in degree, not in state. And although, when named apart, He is called God, He does not thereby constitute two Gods, but one; and that from the very circumstance that He is entitled to be called God, from His union with the Father.

Chapter XX. —The Scriptures Relied on by Praxeas to Support His Heresy But Few. They are Mentioned by Tertullian.

But I must take some further pains to rebut their arguments, when they make selections from the Scriptures in support of their opinion, and refuse to consider the other points, which obviously maintain the rule of faith without any infraction of the unity of the Godhead, and with the full admission of the Monarchy. For as in the Old Testament Scriptures they lay hold of nothing else than, "I am God, and beside me there is no God;" so in the Gospel they simply keep in view the Lord's answer to Philip, "I and my Father are one;" and, "He that hath seen me hath seen the Father; and I am in the Father, and the Father in me." They would have the entire revelation of both Testaments yield to these three passages, whereas the only proper course is to understand the few statements in the light of the many. But in their contention they only act on the principle of all heretics. For, inasmuch as only a few testimonies are to be found (making for them) in the general mass, they pertinaciously set off the few against the many, and assume the later against the earlier. The rule, however, which has been from the beginning established for every case, gives its prescription against the later assumptions, as indeed it also does against the fewer.

Chapter XXI. —In This and the Four Following Chapters It is Shewn, by a Minute Analysis of St. John's Gospel, that the Father and Son are Constantly Spoken of as Distinct Persons.

Consider, therefore, how many passages present their prescriptive authority to you in this very Gospel before this inquiry of Philip, and previous to any discussion on your part. And first of all there comes at once to hand the preamble of John to his Gospel, which shows us what He previously was who had to become flesh. "In the beginning was the Word, and the Word was with God, and the Word was God. He was in the beginning with God: all things were made by Him, and without Him was nothing made." Now, since these words may not be taken otherwise than as they are written, there is without doubt shown to be One who was from the beginning, and also One with whom He always was: one the Word of God, the other God (although the Word is also God, but God regarded as the Son of God, not as the Father); One through whom were all things, Another, by whom were all things. But in what sense we call Him Another we have already often described. In that we called Him Another, we must need imply that He is not identical—not identical indeed, yet not as if separate; Other by dispensation, not by division. He, therefore, who became flesh was not the very same as He from whom the Word came. "His glory was beheld—the glory as of the only-begotten of the Father;" not, (observe,) as of the Father. He "declared" (what was in) "the bosom of the Father alone;" the Father did not divulge the secrets of His own bosom. For this is preceded by another statement: "No man hath seen God at any time." Then, again, when He is designated by John (the Baptist) as "the Lamb of God," He is not described as Himself the same with Him of whom He is the beloved Son. He is, no doubt, ever the Son of God, but yet not He Himself of whom He is the Son. This (divine relationship) Nathanæl at once recognized in Him, even as Peter did on another occasion: "Thou art the Son of God." And He affirmed Himself that they were quite right in their convictions; for He answered Nathanæl: "Because I said, I saw thee under the fig-tree, therefore dost thou believe?" And in the same manner He pronounced Peter to be "blessed," inasmuch as "flesh and blood had not revealed it to him"—that he had perceived the Father— "but the Father which is in heaven." By asserting all this, He determined the distinction which is between the two Persons: that is, the Son then on earth, whom Peter had confessed to be the Son of God; and the Father in heaven, who had revealed to Peter the discovery which he had made, that Christ was the Son of God. When He entered the temple, He called it "His Father's house," speaking as the Son. In His address to Nicodemus He says: "So God loved the world, that He gave His only-begotten Son, that whosoever believeth in Him should not perish, but have everlasting life." And again: "For God sent not His Son into the world to condemn the world, but that the world through Him might be saved. He that believeth on Him is not condemned; but he that believeth not is condemned already, because he hath not believed in the name of the only-begotten Son of God." Moreover, when John (the Baptist) was asked what he happened to know of Jesus, he said: "The Father loveth the Son, and hath given all things into His hand. He that believeth on the Son hath everlasting life; and he that believeth not the Son shall not see life, but the wrath of God abideth on him." Whom, indeed, did He reveal to the woman of Samaria? Was it not "the Messiahs which is called Christ?" And so He showed, of course, that He was not the Father, but the Son; and elsewhere He is expressly called "the Christ, the Son of God," and not the Father. He says, therefore," My meat is to do the will of Him that sent me, and to finish His work;" whilst to the Jews He remarks respecting the cure of the impotent man, "My Father worketh hitherto, and I work." "My Father and I"—these are the Son's words. And it was on this very account that "the Jews sought the more intently to kill Him, not only because He broke the Sabbath, but also because He said that God was His Father, thus making Himself equal with God. Then indeed did He answer and say unto them, The Son can do nothing of Himself, but what He seeth the Father do; for what things so ever He doeth these also doeth the Son likewise. For the Father loveth the Son, and showeth Him all things that He Himself doeth; and He will also show Him greater works than these, that ye may marvel. For as the Father raiseth up the dead and quickeneth them, even so the Son also quickeneth whom He will. For the Father judgeth no man, but hath committed all judgment unto the Son, that all men should honor the Son, even as they honor the Father. He that honoreth not the Son, honoreth not the Father, who hath sent the Son. Verily, verily, I say unto you, He that heareth my words, and believeth on Him that sent me, hath everlasting life, and shall not come into condemnation, but is passed from death unto life. Verily I say unto you, that the hour is coming, when the dead shall hear the voice of the Son of God; and when they have heard it, they shall live. For as the Father hath eternal life in Himself, so also hath He given to the Son to have eternal life in Himself; and He hath given Him authority to execute judgment also, because He is the Son of man"—that is, according to the flesh, even as He is also the Son of God through His Spirit. Afterwards He goes on to say: "But I have greater witness than that of John; for the works which the Father hath given me to finish—those very works bear witness of me that the Father hath sent me. And the Father Himself, which hath sent me, hath also borne witness of me." But He at once adds, "Ye have neither heard His voice at any time, nor seen His shape;" thus affirming that in former times it was not the Father, but the Son, who used to be seen and heard. Then He says at last: "I am come in my Father's name, and ye have not received me." It was therefore always the Son (of whom we read) under the designation of the Almighty and Most High God, and King, and Lord. To those also who inquired "what they should do to work the works of God," He answered, "This is the work of God, that ye believe on Him whom He hath sent." He also declares Himself to be "the bread which the Father sent from heaven;" and adds, that "all that the Father gave Him should come to Him, and that He Himself would not reject them, because He had come down from heaven not to do His own will, but the will of the Father; and that the will of the Father was that everyone who saw the Son, and believed on Him, should obtain the life (everlasting,) and the resurrection at the last day. No man indeed was able to come to Him, except the Father attracted him; whereas everyone who had heard and learnt of the Father came to Him." He goes on then expressly to say, "Not that any man hath seen the Father;" thus showing us that it was through the Word of the Father that men were instructed and taught. Then, when many departed from Him, and He turned to the apostles with the inquiry whether "they also would go away," what was Simon Peter's answer? "To whom shall we go? Thou hast the words of eternal life, and we believe that Thou art the Christ." (Tell me now, did they believe) Him to be the Father, or the Christ of the Father?

Chapter XXII. —Sundry Passages of St. John Quoted, to Show the Distinction Between the Father and the Son. Even Praxeas' Classic Text—I and My Father are One—Shown to Be Against Him.

Again, whose doctrine does He announce, at which all were astonished? Was it His own or the Father's? So, when they were in doubt among themselves whether He were the Christ (not as being the Father, of course but as the Son), He says to them "You are not ignorant whence I am; and I am not come of myself, but He that sent me is true, whom ye know not; but I know Him, because I am from Him." He did not say, Because I myself am He; and, I have sent mine own self: but His words are, "He hath sent me." When, likewise, the Pharisees sent men to apprehend Him, He says: "Yet a little while am I with you, and (then) I go unto Him that sent me." When, however, He declares that He is not alone, and uses these words, "but I and the Father that sent me," does He not show that there are Two—Two, and yet inseparable? Indeed, this was the sum and substance of what He was teaching them, that they were inseparably Two; since, after citing the law when it affirms the truth of two men's testimony, He adds at once: "I am one who am bearing witness of myself; and the Father (is another,) who hath sent me, and beareth witness of me." Now, if He were one—being at once both the Son and the Father—He certainly would not have quoted the sanction of the law, which requires not the testimony of one, but of two. Likewise, when they asked Him where His Father was, He answered them, that they had known neither Himself nor the Father; and in this answer He plainly told them of Two, whom they were ignorant of. Granted that "if they had known Him, they would have known the Father also," this certainly does not imply that He was Himself both Father and Son; but that, by reason of the inseparability of the Two, it was impossible for one of them to be either acknowledged or unknown without the other. "He that sent me," says He, "is true; and I am telling the world those things which I have heard of Him." And the Scripture narrative goes on to explain in an exoteric manner, that "they understood not that He spoke to them concerning the Father," although they ought certainly to have known that the Father's words were uttered in the Son, because they read in Jeremiah, "And the Lord said to me, Behold, I have put my words in thy mouth;" and again in Isaiah, "The Lord hath given to me the tongue of learning that I should understand when to speak a word in season." In accordance with which, Christ Himself says: "Then shall ye know that I am He and that I am saying nothing of my own self; but that, as my Father hath taught me, so I speak, because He that sent me is with me." This also amounts to a proof that they were Two, (although) undivided. Likewise, when upbraiding the Jews in His discussion with them, because they wished to kill Him, He said, "I speak that which I have seen with my Father, and ye do that which ye have seen with your father;" "but now ye seek to kill me, a man that hath told you the truth which I have heard of God;" and again, "If God were your Father, ye would love me, for I proceeded forth and came from God," (still they are not hereby separated, although He declares that He proceeded forth from the Father. Some persons indeed seize the opportunity afforded them in these words to propound their heresy of His separation; but His coming out from God is like the ray's procession from the sun, and the river's from the fountain, and the tree's from the seed); "I have not a devil, but I honor my Father;" again, "If I honor myself, my honor is nothing: it is my Father that honoreth me, of whom ye say, that He is your God: yet ye have not known Him, but I know Him; and if I should say, I know Him not, I shall be a liar like unto you; but I know Him, and keep His saying." But when He goes on to say, "Your father Abraham rejoiced to see my day; and he saw it, and was glad," He certainly proves that it was not the Father that appeared to Abraham, but the Son. In like manner He declares, in the case of the man born blind, "that He must do the works of the Father which had sent Him;" and after He had given the man sight, He said to him, "Dost thou believe in the Son of God?" Then, upon the man's inquiring who He was, He proceeded to reveal Himself to him, as that Son of God whom He had announced to him as the right object of his faith. In a later passage He declares that He is known by the Father, and the Father by Him; adding that He was so wholly loved by the Father, that He was laying down His life, because He had received this commandment from the Father. When He was asked by the Jews if He were the very Christ (meaning, of course, the Christ of God; for to this day the Jews expect not the Father Himself, but the Christ of God, it being nowhere said that the Father will come as the Christ), He said to them, "I am telling you, and yet ye do not believe: the works which I am doing, in my Father's name, they actually bear witness of me." Witness of what? Of that very thing, to be sure, of which they were making inquiry—whether He were the Christ of God. Then, again, concerning His sheep, and (the assurance) that no man should pluck them out of His hand, He says, "My Father, which gave them to me, is greater than all;" adding immediately, "I am and my Father are one." Here, then, they take their stand, too infatuated, nay, too blind, to see in the first place that there is in this passage an intimation of Two Beings— "I and my Father;" then that there is a plural predicate, "are," inapplicable to one person only; and lastly, that (the predicate terminates in an abstract, not a personal noun)— "we are one thing" Unum, not "one person" Unus. For if He had said "one Person," He might have rendered some assistance to their opinion. Unus, no doubt, indicates the singular number; but (here we have a case where) "Two" are still the subject in the masculine gender. He accordingly says Unum, a neuter term, which does not imply singularity of number, but unity of essence, likeness, conjunction, affection on the Father's part, who loves the Son, and submission on the Son's, who obeys the Father's will. When He says, "I and my Father are one" in essence—Unum—He shows that there are Two, whom He puts on an equality and unites in one. He therefore adds to this very statement, that He "had showed them many works from the Father," for none of which did He deserve to be stoned. And to prevent their thinking Him deserving of this fate, as if He had claimed to be considered as God Himself, that is, the Father, by having said, "I and my Father are One," representing Himself as the Father's divine Son, and not as God Himself, He says, "If it is written in your law, I said, Ye are gods; and if the Scripture cannot be broken, say ye of Him whom the Father hath sanctified and sent into the world, that He blasphemeth, because He said, I am the Son of God? If I do not the works of my Father, believe me not; but if I do, even if ye will not believe me, still believe the works; and know that I am in the Father, and the Father in me." It must therefore be by the works that the Father is in the Son, and the Son in the Father; and so it is by the works that we understand that the Father is one with the Son. All along did He therefore strenuously aim at this conclusion, that while they were of one power and essence, they should still be believed to be Two; for otherwise, unless they were believed to be Two, the Son could not possibly be believed to have any existence at all.

Chapter XXIII. —More Passages from the Same Gospel in Proof of the Same Portion of the Catholic Faith. Praxeas' Taunt of Worshipping Two Gods Repudiated.

Again, when Martha in a later passage acknowledged Him to be the Son of God, she no more made a mistake than Peter and Nathanæl had; and yet, even if she had made a mistake, she would at once have learnt the truth: for, behold, when about to raise her brother from the dead, the Lord looked up to heaven, and, addressing the Father, said—as the Son, of course: "Father, I thank Thee that Thou always hearest me; it is because of these crowds that are standing by that I have spoken to Thee, that they may believe that Thou hast sent me." But in the trouble of His soul, (on a later occasion,) He said: "What shall I say? Father, save me from this hour: but for this cause is it that I am come to this hour; only, O Father, do Thou glorify Thy name"—in which He spoke as the Son. (At another time) He said: "I am come in my Father's name." Accordingly, the Son's voice was indeed alone sufficient, (when addressed) to the Father. But, behold, with an abundance (of evidence) the Father from heaven replies, for the purpose of testifying to the Son: "This is my beloved Son, in whom I am well pleased; hear ye Him." So, again, in that asseveration, "I have both glorified, and will glorify again," how many Persons do you discover, obstinate Praxeas? Are there not as many as there are voices? You have the Son on earth, you have the Father in heaven.

Now this is not a separation; it is nothing but the divine dispensation. We know, however, that God is in the bottomless depths, and exists everywhere; but then it is by power and authority. We are also sure that the Son, being indivisible from Him, is everywhere with Him. Nevertheless, in the Economy or Dispensation itself, the Father willed that the Son should be regarded as on earth, and Himself in heaven; whither the Son also Himself looked up, and prayed, and made supplication of the Father; whither also He taught us to raise ourselves, and pray, "Our Father which art in heaven," etc., —although, indeed, He is everywhere present. This heaven the Father willed to be His own throne; while He made the Son to be "a little lower than the angels," by sending Him down to the earth, but meaning at the same time to "crown Him with glory and honor," even by taking Him back to heaven. This He now made good to Him when He said: "I have both glorified Thee, and will glorify Thee again." The Son offers His request from earth, the Father gives His promise from heaven. Why, then, do you make liars of both the Father and the Son? If either the Father spoke from heaven to the Son when He Himself was the Son on earth, or the Son prayed to the Father when He was Himself the Son in heaven, how happens it that the Son made a request of His own very self, by asking it of the Father, since the Son was the Father? Or, on the other hand, how is it that the Father made a promise to Himself, by making it to the Son, since the Father was the Son? Were we even to maintain that they are two separate gods, as you are so fond of throwing out against us, it would be a more tolerable assertion than the maintenance of so versatile and changeful a God as yours! Therefore, it was that in the passage before us the Lord declared to the people present: "Not on my own account has this voice addressed me, but for your sakes," that these likewise may believe both in the Father and in the Son, severally, in their own names and persons and positions. "Then again, Jesus exclaims, and says, He that believeth on me, believeth not on me, but on Him that sent me;" because it is through the Son that men believe in the Father, while the Father also is the authority whence springs belief in the Son. "And he that seeth me, seeth Him that sent me." How so? Even because, (as He afterwards declares,) "I have not spoken from myself, but the Father which sent me: He hath given me a commandment what I should say, and what I should speak." For "the Lord God hath given me the tongue of the learned, that I should know when I ought to speak" the word which I actually speak. "Even as the Father hath said unto me, so do I speak." Now, in what way these things were said to Him, the evangelist and beloved disciple John knew better than Praxeas; and therefore he adds concerning his own meaning: "Now before the feast of the Passover, Jesus knew that the Father had given all things into His hands, and that He had come from God, and was going to God." Praxeas, however, would have it that it was the Father who proceeded forth from Himself, and had returned to Himself; so that what the devil put into the heart of Judas was the betrayal, not of the Son, but of the Father Himself. But for the matter of that, things have not turned out well either for the devil or the heretic; because, even in the Son's case, the treason which the devil wrought against Him contributed nothing to his advantage. It was, then, the Son of God, who was in the Son of man, that was betrayed, as the Scripture says afterwards: "Now is the Son of man glorified, and God is glorified in Him." Who is here meant by "God?" Certainly not the Father, but the Word of the Father, who was in the Son of man—that is in the flesh, in which Jesus had been already glorified by the divine power and word. "And God," says He, "shall also glorify Him in Himself;" that is to say, the Father shall glorify the Son, because He has Him within Himself; and even though prostrated to the earth, and put to death, He would soon glorify Him by His resurrection, and making Him conqueror over death.

Chapter XXIV. —On St. Philip's Conversation with Christ. He that Hath Seen Me, Hath Seen the Father. This Text Explained in an Anti-Praxean Sense.

But there were some who even then did not understand. For Thomas, who was so long incredulous, said: "Lord, we know not whither Thou goest; and how can we know the way? Jesus saith unto him, I am the way, the truth, and the life: no man cometh unto the Father, but by me. If ye had known me, ye would have known the Father also: but henceforth ye know Him, and have seen Him." And now we come to Philip, who, roused with the expectation of seeing the Father, and not understanding in what sense he was to take "seeing the Father," says: "Show us the Father, and it sufficeth us." Then the Lord answered him: "Have I been so long time with you, and yet hast thou not known me, Philip?" Now whom does He say that they ought to have known? —for this is the sole point of discussion. Was it as the Father that they ought to have known Him, or as the Son? If it was as the Father, Praxeas must tell us how Christ, who had been so long time with them, could have possibly ever been (I will not say understood, but even) supposed to have been the Father. He is clearly defined to us in all Scriptures—in the Old Testament as the Christ of God, in the New Testament as the Son of God. In this character was He anciently predicted, in this was He also declared even by Christ Himself; nay, by the very Father also, who openly confesses Him from heaven as His Son, and as His Son glorifies Him. "This is my beloved Son;" "I have glorified Him, and I will glorify Him." In this character, too, was He believed on by His disciples, and rejected by the Jews. It was, moreover, in this character that He wished to be accepted by them whenever He named the Father, and gave preference to the Father, and honored the Father. This, then, being the case, it was not the Father whom, after His lengthened intercourse with them, they were ignorant of, but it was the Son; and accordingly the Lord, while upbraiding Philip for not knowing

Himself who was the object of their ignorance, wished Himself to be acknowledged indeed as that Being whom He had reproached them for being ignorant of after so long a time—in a word, as the Son. And now it may be seen in what sense it was said, "He that hath seen me hath seen the Father,"—even in the same in which it was said in a previous passage, "I and my Father are one." Wherefore? Because "I came forth from the Father, and am come into the world" and, "I am the way: no man cometh unto the Father, but by me;" and, "No man can come to me, except the Father draw him;" and, "All things are delivered unto me by the Father;" and, "As the Father quickeneth (the dead), so also doth the Son;" and again, "If ye had known me, ye would have known the Father also." For in all these passages He had shown Himself to be the Father's Commissioner, through whose agency even the Father could be seen in His works, and heard in His words, and recognized in the Son's administration of the Father's words and deeds. The Father indeed was invisible, as Philip had learnt in the law, and ought at the moment to have remembered: "No man shall see God, and live." So he is reproved for desiring to see the Father, as if He were a visible Being, and is taught that He only becomes visible in the Son from His mighty works, and not in the manifestation of His person. If, indeed, He meant the Father to be understood as the same with the Son, by saying, "He who seeth me seeth the Father," how is it that He adds immediately afterwards, "Believest thou not that I am in the Father, and the Father in me?" He ought rather to have said: "Believest thou not that I am the Father?" With what view else did He so emphatically dwell on this point, if it were not to clear up that which He wished men to understand—namely, that He was the Son? And then, again, by saying, "Believest thou not that I am in the Father, and the Father in me," He laid the greater stress on His question on this very account, that He should not, because He had said, "He that hath seen me, hath seen the Father," be supposed to be the Father; because He had never wished Himself to be so regarded, having always professed

Himself to be the Son, and to have come from the Father. And then He also set the conjunction of the two Persons in the clearest light, in order that no wish might be entertained of seeing the Father as if He were separately visible, and that the Son might be regarded as the representative of the Father. And yet He omitted not to explain how the Father was in the Son and the Son in the Father. "The words," says He, "which I speak unto you, are not mine," because indeed they were the Father's words; "but the Father that dwelleth in me, He doeth the works." It is therefore by His mighty works, and by the words of His doctrine, that the Father who dwells in the Son makes Himself visible—even by those words and works whereby He abides in Him, and also by Him in whom He abides; the special properties of Both the Persons being apparent from this very circumstance, that He says, "I am in the Father, and the Father is in me." Accordingly, He adds: "Believe—" What? That I am the Father? I do not find that it is so written, but rather, "that I am in the Father, and the Father in me; or else believe me for my works' sake;" meaning those works by which the Father manifested Himself to be in the Son, not indeed to the sight of man, but to his intelligence.

Chapter XXV. —The Paraclete, or Holy Ghost. He is Distinct from the Father and the Son as to Their Personal Existence. One and Inseparable from Them as to Their Divine Nature. Other Quotations Out of St. John's Gospel.

What follows Philip's question, and the Lord's whole treatment of it, to the end of John's Gospel, continues to furnish us with statements of the same kind, distinguishing the Father and the Son, with the properties of each. Then there is the Paraclete or Comforter, also, which He promises to pray for to the Father, and to send from heaven after He had ascended to the Father. He is called "another Comforter," indeed; but in what way He is another we have already shown, "He shall receive of mine," says Christ, just as Christ Himself received of the Father's. Thus the connection of the Father in the Son, and of the Son in the Paraclete, produces three coherent Persons, who are yet distinct One from Another. These Three are one essence, not one Person, as it is said, "I and my Father are One," in respect of unity of substance not singularity of number. Run through the whole Gospel, and you will find that He whom you believe to be the Father (described as acting for the Father, although you, for your part, forsooth, suppose that "the Father, being the husbandman," must surely have been on earth) is once more recognized by the Son as in heaven, when, "lifting up His eyes thereto," He commended His disciples to the safe-keeping of the Father. We have, moreover, in that other Gospel a clear revelation, i.e. of the Son's distinction from the Father, "My God, why hast Thou forsaken me?" and again, (in the third Gospel,) "Father, into Thy hands I commend my spirit." But even if (we had not these passages, we meet with satisfactory evidence) after His resurrection and glorious victory over death. Now that all the restraint of His humiliation is taken away, He might, if possible, have shown Himself as the Father to so faithful a woman (as Mary Magdalene) when she approached to touch Him, out of love, not from curiosity, nor with Thomas' incredulity. But not so; Jesus saith unto her, "Touch me not, for I am not yet ascended to my Father; but go to my brethren" (and even in this He proves Himself to be the Son; for if He had been the Father, He would have called them His children, (instead of His brethren), "and say unto them, I ascend unto my Father and your Father, and to my God and your God." Now, does this mean, I ascend as the Father to the Father, and as God to God? Or as the Son to the Father, and as the Word to God? Wherefore also does this Gospel, at its very termination, intimate that these things were ever written, if it be not, to use its own words, "that ye might believe that Jesus Christ is the Son of God?" Whenever, therefore, you take any of the statements of this Gospel, and apply them to demonstrate the identity of the Father and the Son, supposing that they serve your views therein, you are contending against the definite purpose of the Gospel. For these things certainly are not written that you may believe that Jesus Christ is the Father, but the Son.

Chapter XXVI. —A Brief Reference to the Gospels of St. Matthew and St. Luke. Their Agreement with St. John, in Respect to the Distinct Personality of the Father and the Son.

In addition to Philip's conversation, and the Lord's reply to it, the reader will observe that we have run through John's Gospel to show that many other passages of a clear purport, both before and after that chapter, are only in strict accord with that single and prominent statement, which must be interpreted agreeably to all other places, rather than in opposition to them, and indeed to its own inherent and natural sense. I will not here largely use the support of the other Gospels, which confirm our belief by the Lord's nativity: it is sufficient to remark that He who had to be born of a virgin is announced in express terms by the angel himself as the Son of God: "The Spirit of God shall come upon thee, and the power of the Highest shall overshadow thee; therefore, also the Holy Thing that shall be born of thee shall be called the Son of God." On this passage even they will wish to raise a cavil; but truth will prevail. Of course, they say, the Son of God is God, and the power of the highest is the Most High. And they do not hesitate to insinuate what, if it had been true, would have been written. Whom was he so afraid of as not plainly to declare, "God shall come upon thee, and the Highest shall overshadow thee?" Now, by saying "the Spirit of God" (although the Spirit of God is God,) and by not directly naming God, he wished that portion of the whole Godhead to be understood, which was about to retire into the designation of "the Son." The Spirit of God in this passage must be the same as the Word. For just as, when John says, "The Word was made flesh," we understand the Spirit also in the mention of the Word: so here, too, we acknowledge the Word likewise in the name of the Spirit. For both the Spirit is the substance of the Word, and the Word is the operation of the Spirit, and the Two are One (and the same). Now John must mean One when he speaks of Him as "having been made flesh," and the angel Another when he announces Him as "about to be born," if the Spirit is not the Word, and the Word the Spirit. For just as the Word of God is not actually He whose Word He is, so also the Spirit (although He is called God) is not actually He whose Spirit He is said to be. Nothing which belongs to something else is actually the very same thing as that to which it belongs. Clearly, when anything proceeds from a personal subject, and so belongs to him, since it comes from him, it may possibly be such in quality exactly as the personal subject himself is from whom it proceeds, and to whom it belongs. And thus the Spirit is God, and the Word is God, because proceeding from God, but yet is not actually the very same as He from whom He proceeds. Now that which is God of God, although He is an actually existing thing, yet He cannot be God Himself (exclusively), but so far God as He is of the same substance as God Himself, and as being an actually existing thing, and as a portion of the Whole. Much more will "the power of the Highest" not be the Highest Himself, because It is not an actually existing thing, as being Spirit—in the same way as the wisdom (of God) and the providence (of God) is not God: these attributes are not substances, but the accidents of the particular substance. Power is incidental to the Spirit, but cannot itself be the Spirit. These things, therefore, whatsoever they are— (I mean) the Spirit of God, and the Word and the Power—having been conferred on the Virgin, that which is born of her is the Son of God. This He Himself, in those other Gospels also, testifies Himself to have been from His very boyhood: "Wist ye not," says He, "that I must be about my Father's business?" Satan likewise knew Him to be this in his temptations: "Since Thou art the Son of God." This, accordingly, the devils also acknowledge Him to be: "we know Thee, who Thou art, the Holy Son of God." His "Father" He Himself adores. When acknowledged by Peter as the "Christ (the Son) of God," He does not deny the relation. He exults in spirit when He says to the Father, "I thank Thee, O Father, because Thou hast hid these things from the wise and prudent." He, moreover, affirms also that to no man is the Father known, but to His Son; and promises that, as the Son of the Father, He will confess those who confess Him, and deny those who deny Him, before His Father. He also introduces a parable of the mission to the vineyard of the Son (not the Father), who was sent after so many servants, and slain by the husbandmen, and avenged by the Father. He is also ignorant of the last day and hour, which is known to the Father only. He awards the kingdom to His disciples, as He says it had been appointed to Himself by the Father. He has power to ask, if He will, legions of angels from the Father for His help. He exclaims that God had forsaken Him. He commends His spirit into the hands of the Father. After His resurrection He promises in a pledge to His disciples that He will send them the promise of His Father; and lastly, He commands them to baptize into the Father and the Son and the Holy Ghost, not into a unipersonal God. And indeed it is not once only, but three times, that we are immersed into the Three Persons, at each several mention of Their names.

Chapter XXVII. —The Distinction of the Father and the Son, Thus Established, He Now Proves the Distinction of the Two Natures, Which Were, Without Confusion, United in the Person of the Son. The Subterfuges of Praxeas Thus Exposed.

But why should I linger over matters which are so evident, when I ought to be attacking points on which they seek to obscure the plainest proof? For, confuted on all sides on the distinction between the Father and the Son, which we maintain without destroying their inseparable union—as (by the examples) of the sun and the ray, and the fountain and the river—yet, by help of (their conceit) an indivisible number, (with issues) of two and three, they endeavor to interpret this distinction in a way which shall nevertheless tally with their own opinions: so that, all in one Person, they distinguish two, Father and Son, understanding the Son to be flesh, that is man, that is Jesus; and the Father to be spirit, that is God, that is Christ. Thus they, while contending that the Father and the Son are one and the same, do in fact begin by dividing them rather than uniting them. For if Jesus is one, and Christ is another, then the Son will be different from the Father, because the Son is Jesus, and the Father is Christ. Such a monarchy as this they learnt, I suppose, in the school of Valentinus, making two—Jesus and Christ. But this conception of theirs has been, in fact, already confuted in what we have previously advanced, because the Word of God or the Spirit of God is also called the power of the Highest, whom they make the Father; whereas these relations are not themselves the same as He whose relations they are said to be, but they proceed from Him and appertain to Him. However, another refutation awaits them on this point of their heresy. See, say they, it was announced by the angel: "Therefore that Holy Thing which shall be born of thee shall be called the Son of God." Therefore, (they argue,) as it was the flesh that was born, it must be the flesh that is the Son of God. Nay, (I answer,) this is spoken concerning the Spirit of God. For it was certainly of the Holy Spirit that the virgin conceived; and that which He conceived, she brought forth. That, therefore, had to be born which was conceived and was to be brought forth; that is to say, the Spirit, whose "name should be called Emmanuel which, being interpreted, is, God with us." Besides, the flesh is not God, so that it could not have been said concerning it, "That Holy Thing shall be called the Son of God," but only that Divine Being who was born in the flesh, of whom the psalm also says, "Since God became man in the midst of it, and established it by the will of the Father." Now what Divine Person was born in it? The Word, and the Spirit which became incarnate with the Word by the will of the Father. The Word, therefore, is incarnate; and this must be the point of our inquiry: How the Word became flesh—whether it was by having been transfigured, as it were, in the flesh, or by having really clothed Himself in flesh. Certainly it was by a real clothing of Himself in flesh. For the rest, we must need believe God to be unchangeable, and incapable of form, as being eternal. But transfiguration is the destruction of that which previously existed. For whatsoever is transfigured into some other thing ceases to be that which it had been, and begins to be that which it previously was not. God, however, neither ceases to be what He was, nor can He be any other thing than what He is. The Word is God, and "the Word of the Lord remaineth forever,"—even by holding on unchangeably in His own proper form. Now, if He admits not of being transfigured, it must follow that He be understood in this sense to have become flesh, when He comes to be in the flesh, and is manifested, and is seen, and is handled by means of the flesh; since all the other points likewise require to be thus understood. For if the Word became flesh by a transfiguration and change of substance, it follows at once that Jesus must be a substance compounded of two substances—of flesh and spirit—a kind of mixture, like electrum, composed of gold and silver; and it begins to be neither gold (that is to say, spirit) nor silver (that is to say, flesh)—the one being changed by the other, and a third substance produced. Jesus, therefore, cannot at this rate be God for He has ceased to be the Word, which was made flesh; nor can He be Man incarnate for He is not properly flesh, and it was flesh which the Word became. Being compounded, therefore, of both, He actually is neither; He is rather some third substance, very different from either. But the truth is, we find that He is expressly set forth as both God and Man; the very psalm which we have quoted intimating (of the flesh), that "God became Man in the midst of it, He therefore established it by the will of the Father,"—certainly in all respects as the Son of God and the Son of Man, being God and Man, differing no doubt according to each substance in its own especial property, inasmuch as the Word is nothing else but God, and the flesh

nothing else but Man. Thus does the apostle also teach respecting His two substances, saying, "who was made of the seed of David;" in which words He will be Man and Son of Man. "Who was declared to be the Son of God, according to the Spirit;" in which words He will be God, and the Word—the Son of God. We see plainly the twofold state, which is not confounded, but conjoined in One Person—Jesus, God and Man. Concerning Christ, indeed, I defer what I have to say. (I remark here), that the property of each nature is so wholly preserved, that the Spirit on the one hand did all things in Jesus suitable to Itself, such as miracles, and mighty deeds, and wonders; and the Flesh, on the other hand, exhibited the affections which belong to it. It was hungry under the devil's temptation, thirsty with the Samaritan woman, wept over Lazarus, was troubled even unto death, and at last actually died. If, however, it was only a tertium quid, some composite essence formed out of the Two substances, like the electrum (which we have mentioned), there would be no distinct proofs apparent of either nature. But by a transfer of functions, the Spirit would have done things to be done by the Flesh, and the Flesh such as are effected by the Spirit; or else such things as are suited neither to the Flesh nor to the Spirit, but confusedly of some third character. Nay more, on this supposition, either the Word underwent death, or the flesh did not die, if so be the Word was converted into flesh; because either the flesh was immortal, or the Word was mortal. Forasmuch, however, as the two substances acted distinctly, each in its own character, there necessarily accrued to them severally their own operations, and their own issues. Learn then, together with Nicodemus, that "that which is born in the flesh is flesh, and that which is born of the Spirit is Spirit." Neither the flesh becomes Spirit, nor the Spirit flesh. In one Person they no doubt are well able to be co-existent. Of them Jesus consists—Man, of the flesh; of the Spirit, God—and the angel designated Him as "the Son of God," in respect of that nature, in which He was Spirit, reserving for the flesh the appellation "Son of Man." In like manner, again, the apostle calls Him "the Mediator between God and Men," and so affirmed His participation of both substances. Now, to end the matter, will you, who interpret the Son of God to be flesh, be so good as to show us what the Son of Man is? Will He then, I want to know, be the Spirit? But you insist upon it that the Father Himself is the Spirit, on the ground that "God is a Spirit," just as if we did not read also that there is "the Spirit of God;" in the same manner as we find that as "the Word was God," so also there is "the Word of God."

Chapter XXVIII. —Christ Not the Father, as Praxeas Said. The Inconsistency of This Opinion, No Less Than Its Absurdity, Exposed. The True Doctrine of Jesus Christ According to St. Paul, Who Agrees with Other Sacred Writers.

And so, most foolish heretic, you make Christ to be the Father, without once considering the actual force of this name, if indeed Christ is a name, and not rather a surname, or designation; for it signifies "Anointed." But Anointed is no more a proper name than Clothed or Shod; it is only an accessory to a name. Suppose now that by some means Jesus were also called Vestitus (Clothed), as He is actually called Christ from the mystery of His anointing, would you in like manner say that Jesus was the Son of God, and at the same time suppose that Vestitus was the Father? Now then, concerning Christ, if Christ is the Father, the Father is an Anointed One, and receives the unction of course from another. Else if it is from Himself that He receives it, then you must prove it to us. But we learn no such fact from the Acts of the Apostles in that ejaculation of the Church to God, "Of a truth, Lord, against Thy Holy Child Jesus, whom Thou hast anointed, both Herod and Pontius Pilate with the Gentiles and the people of Israel were gathered together." These then testified both that Jesus was the Son of God, and that being the Son, He was anointed by the Father. Christ therefore must be the same as Jesus who was anointed by the Father, and not the Father, who anointed the Son. To the same effect are the words of Peter: "Let all the house of Israel know assuredly that God hath made that same Jesus, whom ye have crucified, both Lord and Christ," that is, Anointed. John, moreover, brands that man as "a liar" who "denieth that Jesus is the Christ;" whilst on the other hand he declares that "everyone is born of God who believeth that Jesus is the Christ." Wherefore he also exhorts us to believe in the name of His (the Father's,) Son Jesus Christ, that "our fellowship may be with the Father, and with His Son Jesus Christ." Paul, in like manner, everywhere speaks of "God the Father, and our Lord Jesus Christ." When writing to the Romans, he gives thanks to God through our Lord Jesus Christ. To the Galatians he declares himself to be "an apostle not of men, neither by man, but through Jesus Christ and God the Father." You possess indeed all his writings, which testify plainly to the same effect, and set forth Two—God the Father, and our Lord Jesus Christ, the Son of the Father. (They also testify) that Jesus is Himself the Christ, and under one or the other designation the Son of God. For precisely by the same right as both names belong to the same Person, even the Son of God, does either name alone without the other belong to the same Person. Consequently, whether it be the name Jesus which occurs alone, Christ is also understood, because Jesus is the Anointed One; or if the name Christ is the only one given, then Jesus is identified with Him, because the Anointed One is Jesus. Now, of these two names Jesus Christ, the former is the proper one, which was given to Him by the angel; and the latter is only an adjunct, predicable of Him from His anointing—thus suggesting the proviso that Christ must be the Son, not the Father. How blind, to be sure, is the man who fails to perceive that by the name of Christ some other God is implied, if he ascribes to the Father this name of Christ! For if Christ is God the Father, when He says, "I ascend unto my Father and your Father, and to my God and your God," He of course shows plainly enough that there is above Himself another Father and another God. If, again, the Father is Christ, He must be some other Being who "strengtheneth the thunder, and createth the wind, and declareth unto men His Christ." And if "the kings of the earth stood up, and the rulers were gathered together against the Lord and against His Christ," that Lord must be another Being, against whose Christ were gathered together the kings and the rulers. And if, to quote another passage, "Thus saith the Lord to my Lord Christ," the Lord who speaks to the Father of Christ must be a distinct Being. Moreover, when the apostle in his epistle prays, "That the God of our Lord Jesus Christ may give unto you the spirit of wisdom and of knowledge," He must be other (than Christ), who is the God of Jesus Christ, the bestower of spiritual gifts. And once for all, that we may not wander through every passage, He "who raised up Christ from the dead, and is also to raise up our mortal bodies," must certainly be, as the quickener, different from the dead Father, or even from the quickened Father, if Christ who died is the Father.

Chapter XXIX. —It Was Christ that Died. The Father is Incapable of Suffering Either Solely or with Another. Blasphemous Conclusions Spring from Praxeas' Premises.

Silence! Silence on such blasphemy. Let us be content with saying that Christ died, the Son of the Father; and let this suffice, because the Scriptures have told us so much. For even the apostle, to his declaration—which he makes not without feeling the weight of it—that "Christ died," immediately adds, "according to the Scriptures," in order that he may alleviate the harshness of the statement by the authority of the Scriptures, and so remove offence from the reader. Now, although when two substances are alleged to be in Christ—namely, the divine and the human—it plainly follows that the divine nature is immortal, and that which is human is mortal, it is manifest in what sense he declares "Christ died"—even in the sense in which He was flesh and Man and the Son of Man, not as being the Spirit and the Word and the Son of God. In short, since he says that it was Christ (that is, the Anointed One) that died, he shows us that that which died was the nature which was anointed; in a word, the flesh. Very well, say you; since we on our side affirm our doctrine in precisely the same terms which you use on your side respecting the Son, we are not guilty of blasphemy against the Lord God, for we do not maintain that He died after the divine nature, but only after the human. Nay, but you do blaspheme; because you allege not only that the Father died, but that He died the death of the cross. For "cursed are they which are hanged on a tree,"—a curse which, after the law, is compatible to the Son (inasmuch as "Christ has been made a curse for us," but certainly not the Father); since, however, you convert Christ into the Father, you are chargeable with blasphemy against the Father. But when we assert that Christ was crucified, we do not malign Him with a curse; we only reaffirm the curse pronounced by the law: nor indeed did the apostle utter blasphemy when he said the same thing as we. Besides, as there is no blasphemy in predicating of the subject that which is fairly applicable to it; so, on the other hand, it is blasphemy when that is alleged concerning the subject which is unsuitable to it. On this principle, too, the Father was not associated in suffering with the Son. The heretics, indeed, fearing to incur direct blasphemy against the Father, hope to diminish it by this expedient: they grant us so far that the Father and the Son are Two; adding that, since it is the Son indeed who suffers, the Father is only His fellow-sufferer. But how absurd are they even in this conceit! For what is the meaning of "fellow-suffering," but the endurance of suffering along with another? Now if the Father is incapable of suffering, He. is incapable of suffering in company with another; otherwise, if He can suffer with another, He is of course capable of suffering. You, in fact, yield Him nothing by this subterfuge of your fears. You are afraid to say that He is capable of suffering whom you make to be capable of fellow-suffering. Then, again, the Father is as incapable of fellow-suffering as the Son even is of suffering under the conditions of

His existence as God. Well, but how could the Son suffer, if the Father did not suffer with Him? My answer is, The Father is separate from the Son, though not from Him as God. For even if a river be soiled with mire and mud, although it flows from the fountain identical in nature with it, and is not separated from the fountain, yet the injury which affects the stream reaches not to the fountain; and although it is the water of the fountain which suffers down the stream, still, since it is not affected at the fountain, but only in the river, the fountain suffers nothing, but only the river which issues from the fountain. So likewise the Spirit of God, whatever suffering it might be capable of in the Son, yet, inasmuch as it could not suffer in the Father, the fountain of the Godhead, but only in the Son, it evidently could not have suffered, as the Father. But it is enough for me that the Spirit of God suffered nothing as the Spirit of God, since all that It suffered It suffered in the Son. It was quite another matter for the Father to suffer with the Son in the flesh. This likewise has been treated by us. Nor will anyone deny this, since even we are ourselves unable to suffer for God, unless the Spirit of God be in us, who also utters by our instrumentality whatever pertains to our own conduct and suffering; not, however, that He Himself suffers in our suffering, only He bestows on us the power and capacity of suffering.

Chapter XXX—How the Son Was Forsaken by the Father Upon the Cross. The True Meaning Thereof Fatal to Praxeas. So Too, the Resurrection of Christ, His Ascension, Session at the Father's Right Hand, and Mission of the Holy Ghost.

However, if you persist in pushing your views further, I shall find means of answering you with greater stringency, and of meeting you with the exclamation of the Lord Himself, so as to challenge you with the question, what is your inquiry and reasoning about that? You have Him exclaiming in the midst of His passion: "My God, my God, why hast Thou forsaken me?" Either, then, the Son suffered, being "forsaken" by the Father, and the Father consequently suffered nothing, inasmuch as He forsook the Son; or else, if it was the Father who suffered, then to what God was it that He addressed His cry? But this was the voice of flesh and soul, that is to say, of man—not of the Word and Spirit, that is to say, not of God; and it was uttered so as to prove the impassibility of God, who "forsook" His Son, so far as He handed over His human substance to the suffering of death. This verity the apostle also perceived, when he writes to this effect: "If the Father spared not His own Son." This did Isaiah before him likewise perceive, when he declared: "And the Lord hath delivered Him up for our offences." In this manner He "forsook" Him, in not sparing Him; "forsook" Him, in delivering Him up. In all other respects the Father did not forsake the Son, for it was into His Father's hands that the Son commended His spirit. Indeed, after so commending it, He instantly died; and as the Spirit remained with the flesh, the flesh cannot undergo the full extent of death, i.e., in corruption and decay. For the Son, therefore, to die, amounted to His being forsaken by the Father. The Son, then, both dies and rises again, according to the Scriptures. It is the Son, too, who ascends to the heights of heaven, and also descends to the inner parts of the earth. "He sitteth at the Father's right hand"—not the Father at His own. He is seen by Stephen, at his martyrdom by stoning, still sitting at the right hand of God where He will continue to sit, until the Father shall make His enemies His footstool. He will come again on the clouds of heaven, just as He appeared when He ascended into heaven. Meanwhile He has received from the Father the promised gift, and has shed it forth, even the Holy Spirit—the Third Name in the Godhead, and the Third Degree of the Divine Majesty; the Declarer of the One Monarchy of God, but at the same time the Interpreter of the Economy, to everyone who hears and receives the words of the new prophecy; and "the Leader into all truth," such as is in the Father, and the Son, and the Holy Ghost, according to the mystery of the doctrine of Christ.

Chapter XXXI. —Retrograde Character of the Heresy of Praxeas. The Doctrine of the Blessed Trinity Constitutes the Great Difference Between Judaism and Christianity.

But, (this doctrine of yours bears a likeness) to the Jewish faith, of which this is the substance—so to believe in One God as to refuse to reckon the Son besides Him, and after the Son the Spirit. Now, what difference would there be between us and them, if there were not this distinction which you are for breaking down? What need would there be of the gospel, which is the substance of the New Covenant, laying down (as it does) that the Law and the Prophets lasted until John the Baptist, if thenceforward the Father, the Son, and the Spirit are not both believed in as Three, and as making One Only God? God was pleased to renew His covenant with man in such a way as that His Unity might be believed in, after a new manner, through the Son and the Spirit, in order that God might now be known openly, in His proper Names and Persons, who in ancient times was not plainly understood, though declared through the Son and the Spirit. Away, then, with those "Antichrists who deny the Father and the Son." For they deny the Father, when they say that He is the same as the Son; and they deny the Son, when they suppose Him to be the same as the Father, by assigning to Them things which are not Theirs, and taking away from Them things which are Theirs. But "whosoever shall confess that (Jesus) Christ is the Son of God" (not the Father), "God dwelleth in him, and he in God." We believe not the testimony of God in which He testifies to us of His Son. "He that hath not the Son, hath not life." And that man has not the Son, who believes Him to be any other than the Son.

Postscript

The learned Dr. Holmes, the translator of the Second volume of the Edinburgh series, to which our arrangement has given another position, furnished it with a Preface as follows:

"This volume contains all Tertullian's polemical works (placed in his second volume by Oehler, whose text we have followed), with the exception of the long treatise Against Marcion, which has already formed a volume of this series, and the Adversus Judæos, which, not to increase the bulk of the present volume, appears among the Miscellaneous Tracts.

"For the scanty facts connected with our author's life, and for some general remarks on the importance and style of his writings, the reader is referred to the Introduction of my translation of the Five Books against Marcion.

"The treatises which comprise this volume will be found replete with the vigorous thought and terse expression which always characterize Tertullian.

"Brief synopses are prefixed to the several treatises, and headings are supplied to the chapters: these, with occasional notes on difficult passages and obscure allusions, will, it is hoped, afford sufficient aid for an intelligent perusal of these ancient writings, which cannot fail to be interesting alike to the theologian and the general reader,—full as they are of reverence for revealed truth, and at the same time of independence of judgment, adorned with admirable variety and fullness of knowledge, genial humor, and cultivated imagination."

Elucidations. I.

(Sundry doctrinal statements of Tertullian. See p. 601 (et seqq.), supra.)

I am glad for many reasons that Dr. Holmes appends the following from Bishop Kaye's Account of the Writings of Tertullian:

"On the doctrine of the blessed Trinity, in order to explain his meaning Tertullian borrows illustrations from natural objects. The three Persons of the Trinity stand to each other in the relation of the root, the shrub, and the fruit; of the fountain, the river, and the cut from the river; of the sun, the ray, and the terminating point of the ray. For these illustrations he professes himself indebted to the Revelations of the Paraclete. In later times, divines have occasionally resorted to similar illustrations for the purpose of familiarizing the doctrine of the Trinity to the mind; nor can any danger arise from the proceeding, so long as we recollect that they are illustrations, not arguments—that we must not draw conclusions from them, or think that whatever may be truly predicated of the illustrations, may be predicated with equal truth of that which it was designed to illustrate."

"'Notwithstanding, however, the intimate union which subsists between the Father, Son, and Holy Ghost, we must be careful,' says Tertullian, 'to distinguish between their Persons.' In his representations of this distinction he sometimes uses expressions which in after times, when controversy had introduced greater precision of language, were studiously avoided by the orthodox. Thus he calls the Father the whole substance—the Son a derivation from or portion of the whole."

"After showing that Tertullian's opinions were generally coincident with the orthodox belief of the Christian Church on the great subject of the Trinity in Unity, Bp. Kaye goes on to say: 'We are far from meaning to assert that expressions may not occasionally be found which are capable of a different interpretation, and which were carefully avoided by the orthodox writers of later times, when the controversies respecting the Trinity had introduced greater precision of language.' Pamelius thought it necessary to put the reader on his guard against certain of these expressions; and Semler has noticed, with a sort of ill-natured industry (we call it ill-natured industry, because the true mode of ascertaining a writer's opinions is, not to fix upon particular expressions, but to take the general tenor of his language), every passage in the Tract against Praxeas in which there is any appearance of contradiction, or which will bear a construction favorable to the Arian tenets. Bp. Bull also, who conceives the language of Tertullian to be explicit and correct on the subject of the pre-existence and the consubstantiality, admits that he occasionally uses expressions at variance with the coeternity of Christ. For instance, in the Tract against Hermogenes, we find a passage in which it is expressly asserted that there was a time when the Son was not. Perhaps, however, a reference to the peculiar tenets of Hermogenes will enable us to account for this assertion. That heretic affirmed that matter was eternal, and argued thus: 'God was always God, and always Lord; but the word Lord implies the existence of something over which He was Lord. Unless, therefore, we suppose the eternity of something distinct from God, it is not true that He was always Lord.' Tertullian boldly answered, that God was not always Lord; and that in Scripture we do not find Him called Lord until the work of creation was completed. In like manner, he contended that the titles of Judge and Father imply the existence of sin, and of a Son. As, therefore, there was a time when neither sin nor the Son existed, the titles of Judge and Father were not at that time applicable to God. Tertullian could scarcely mean to affirm (in direct opposition to his own statements in the Tract against Praxeas) that there was ever a time when the λόγος, or Ratio, or Sermo Internus did not exist. But with respect to Wisdom and the Son (Sophia and Filius) the case is different. Tertullian assigns to both a beginning of existence: Sophia was created or formed in order to devise the plan of the universe; and the Son was begotten in order to carry that plan into effect. Bp. Bull appears to have given an accurate representation of the matter, when he says that, according to our author, the Reason and Spirit of God, being the substance of the Word and Son, were coeternal with God; but that the titles of Word and Son were not strictly applicable until the former had been emitted to arrange, and the latter begotten to execute, the work of creation. Without, therefore, attempting to explain, much less to defend, all Tertullian's expressions and reasonings, we are disposed to acquiesce in the statement given by Bp. Bull of his opinions (Defense of the Nicene Creed, sec. iii. ch. x. (p. 545 of the Oxford translation)): 'From all this it is clear how rashly, as usual, Petavius has pronounced that, "so far as relates to the eternity of the Word, it is manifest that Tertullian did not by any means acknowledge it."' To myself, indeed, and as I suppose to my reader also, after the many clear testimonies which I have adduced, the very opposite is manifest, unless indeed Petavius played on the term, the Word, which I will not suppose. For Tertullian does indeed teach that the Son of God was made and was called the Word (Verbumor Sermo) from some definite beginning, i.e.at the time when He went out from God the Father with the voice, 'Let there be light' in order to arrange the universe. But, for all that, that he really believed that the very hypostasis which is called the Word and Son of God is eternal, I have, I think, abundantly demonstrated." (The whole of Bp. Bull's remark is worth considering; it occurs in the translation just referred to, pp. 508–545.)— (Pp. 521–525.)

"In speaking also of the Holy Ghost, Tertullian occasionally uses terms of a very ambiguous and equivocal character. He says, for instance (Adversus Praxean, c. xii.), that in Gen. i. 26, God addressed the Son, His Word (the Second Person in the Trinity), and the Spirit in the Word (the Third Person of the Trinity). Here the distinct personality of the Spirit is expressly asserted; although it is difficult to reconcile Tertullian's words, 'Spiritus in Sermone,' with the assertion. It is, however, certain both from the general tenor of the Tract against Praxeas, and from many passages in his other writings (for instance, Ad Martyras, iii.), that the distinct personality of the Holy Ghost formed an article of Tertullian's creed. The occasional ambiguity of his language respecting the Holy Ghost is perhaps in part to be traced to the variety of senses in which the term 'Spiritus' is used. It is applied generally to God, for 'God is a Spirit' (Adv. Marcionem, ii. 9); and for the same reason to the Son, who is frequently called 'the Spirit of God,' and 'the Spirit of the Creator' (De Oratione, i.; Adv. Praxean, xiv., xxvi.; Adv. Marcionem, v. 8; Apolog.xxiii.; Adv. Marcionem, iii. 6, iv. 33). Bp. Bull likewise (Defense of the Nicene Creed, i. 2), following Grotius, has shown that the word 'Spiritus' is employed by the fathers to express the divine nature in Christ."— (Pp. 525, 526.)

II.

(The bishop of Rome, cap. i. p. 597.)

Probably Victor (a.d.190), who is elsewhere called Victorinus, as Oehler conjectures, by a blunderer who tacked the inus to his name, because he was thinking of Zephyrinus, his immediate successor. This Victor "acknowledged the prophetic gifts of Montanus," and kept up communion with the Phrygian churches that adopted them: but worse than that, he now seems to have patronized the Patri-passion heresy, under the compulsion of Praxeas. So Tertullian says, who certainly had no idea that the Bishop of Rome was the infallible judge of controversies, when he recorded the facts of this strange history. Thus, we find the very founder of "Latin Christianity," accusing a contemporary Bishop of Rome of heresy and the patronage of heresy, in two particulars. Our earliest acquaintance with that See presents us with Polycarp's superior authority, at Rome itself, in maintaining apostolic doctrine and suppressing heresy. "He it was, who coming to Rome," says Irenæus, "in the time of Anicetus, caused many to turn away from the aforesaid heretics (viz. Valentinus and Marcion) to the Church of God, proclaiming that he had received this one and sole truth from the Apostles." Anicetus was a pious prelate who never dreamed of asserting a superior claim as the chief depositary of Apostolic orthodoxy, and whose beautiful example in the Easter-questions discussed between Polycarp and himself, is another illustration of the independence of the sister churches, at that period. Nor is it unworthy to be noted, that the next event, in Western history, establishes a like principle against that other and less worthy occupant of the Roman See, of whom we have spoken. Irenæus rebukes Victor for his dogmatism about Easter, and reproaches him with departing from the example of his predecessors in the same See. With Eleutherus he had previously remonstrated, though mildly, for his toleration of heresy and his patronage of the raising schism of Montanus.

III.

(These three are one, cap. xxv. p. 621. Also p. 606.)

Porson having spoken Pontifically upon the matter of the text of "the Three Witnesses," cadit quæstio, locutus est Augur Apollo. It is of more importance that Bishop Kaye in his calm wisdom, remarks as follows; "In my opinion, the passage in Tertullian, far from containing an allusion to 1 John v. 7, furnishes most decisive proof that he knew nothing of the verse." After this, and the acquiescence of scholars generally, it would be presumption to say a word on the question of quoting it as Scripture. In Textual Criticism it seems to be an established canon that it has no place in the Greek Testament. I submit, however, that, something remains to be said for it, on the ground of the old African Version used and quoted by

Tertullian and Cyprian; and I dare to say, that, while there would be no ground whatever for inserting it in our English Version, the question of striking it out is a widely different one. It would be sacrilege, in my humble opinion, for reasons which will appear, in the following remarks, upon our author.

It appears to me very clear that Tertullian is quoting 1 John v. 7 in the passage now under consideration: "Qui tres unum sunt, non unus, quomodo dictum est, Ego et Pater unum sumus, etc." Let me refer to a work containing a sufficient answer to Porson, on this point of Tertullian's quotation, which it is easier to pass sub-silentio, than to refute. I mean Forster's New Plea, of which the full title is placed in the margin. The whole work is worth thoughtful study, but, I name it with reference to this important passage of our author, exclusively. In connection with other considerations on which I have no right to enlarge in this place, it satisfies me as to the primitive origin of the text in the Vulgate, and hence of its right to stand in our English Vulgate until it can be shewn that the Septuagint Version, quoted and honored by our Lord, is free from similar readings, and divergences from the Hebrew mss.

Stated as a mere question as to the early African Church, the various versions known as the Itala, and the right of the Latin and English Vulgates to remain as they are, the whole question is a fresh one. Let me be pardoned for saying: (1) that I am not pleading for it as a proof-text of the Trinity, having never once quoted it as such in a long ministry, during which I have preached nearly a hundred Trinity-Sunday Sermons; (2) that I consider it as practically Apocryphal, and hence as coming under St. Jerome's law, and being useless to establish doctrine; and (3) that I feel no need of it, owing to the wealth of Scripture on the same subject. Tertullian, himself says that he cites "only a few out of many texts—not pretending to bring up all the passages of Scripture…having produced an accumulation of witnesses in the fullness of their dignity and authority."

To those interested in the question let me commend the learned dissertation of Grabe on the textual case, as it stood in his day. I value it chiefly because it proves that the Greek Testament, elsewhere says, disjointedly, what is collected into 1 John v. 7. It is, therefore, Holy Scripture in substance, if not in the letter. What seems to me important, however, is the balance it gives to the whole context, and the defective character of the grammar and logic, if it be stricken out. In the Septuagint and the Latin Vulgate of the Old Testament we have a precisely similar case. Refer to Psa. xiii., alike in the Latin and the Greek, as compared with our English Version. Between the third and fourth verses, three whole verses are interpolated: Shall we strike them out? Of course, if certain critics are to prevail over St. Paul, for he quotes them (Rom. iii. 10) with the formula: "As it is written." Now, then, till we expurgate the English Version of the Epistle to the Romans,—or rather the original of St. Paul himself, I employ Grabe's argument only to prove my point, which is this, viz., that 1 John v. 7being Scripture, ought to be left untouched in the Versions where it stands, although it be no part of the Greek Testament.

www.ingramcontent.com/pod-product-compliance
Ingram Content Group UK Ltd.
Pitfield, Milton Keynes, MK11 3LW, UK
UKHW020135250726
13967UKWH00002B/675

The ease with which he lifted her up made her mouth water. The sane part of her mind groaned disapprovingly.

"*Habibi*, let's not fight. Maybe you just need a reminder of how I make you feel?" Samir liked the chase, but chasing without reward was just frustration. He lived for a good hard fuck in a pussy as exquisite as hers had to be. While he was a patient man, patience was only a virtue for so long. He stood, even as his help entered and placed the steak and rice dishes on an oaken side table. Coming around to Amanda's side, he leaned down, and with his fingers unfastened the jeweled veil, wanting to see his future lover without the masking effects of the silk.

Her hair, a fiery auburn that matched his desires, was swept up into a bun with softly curled tendrils raining from it. Her coloring was set off by silver combs adorned with emeralds and white rose petals in her hair. She was a peerless beauty, a figure from a fairy tale, a goddess.

Leaning in further, Samir kissed the pulse point just below her right earlobe. "You, Amanda, are perfect. Has anyone ever told you that?"

BOOKS BY MONTANA NIGHT

BILLIONAIRE BROTHERS: HAMILTON

The Russian Mail-Order Bride
The Stand-In Bride
The Tycoon's Replacement Bride Part 1
The Tycoon's Replacement Bride Part 2
The Tycoon's Replacement Bride Part 3

Visit the author's website for special offers and updates:

montananight.labelleauboisdormant.co.uk